Policy and Publics:

Leisure, Culture

and Commerce

Edited by

Peter Bramham

Wilf Murphy

LSA

Publication No. 65

0906337755

First published in 1999 by
Leisure Studies Association

The collection as a whole © 1999 LSA
The individual contributions © 1999 the respective authors

A catalogue record for this book
is available from the British Library.

ISBN: 0 906337 75 5

Layout design and typesetting by Myrene L. McFee
Reproduction by University of Brighton
Binding by Kensett Ltd., Hove

Contents

Notes on the Contributors

Peter Bramham

Peter Bramham trained as a sociologist and completed a PhD in criminology. His teaching and research have focused on youth, lifestyles and on leisure policy issues. His working life has been spent (mainly with John Spink) in West Yorkshire, both in Bradford and in Leeds, and recent work has centred on the impact of deindustrialisation and the development of postmodern responses to urban change in northern provincial cities. More recently he has been involved in a research project with Dr. Anne Flintoff investigating active lifestyles amongst year 10 pupils in a sample of Leeds schools. He is currently based in the School of Leisure and Sport Studies as Senior Lecturer in Leisure at Leeds Metropolitan University, teaching modules in leisure policy and the leisure theory and supervising research into policy communities, race and ethnicity in sport.

Sylvia Harvey

Sylvia Harvey is Reader in Broadcasting Policy at Sheffield Hallam University, currently researching the concept of impartiality, with a comparative focus on the different broadcasting traditions of Britain and the United States. She has served on various advisory bodies for the Arts Council and the British Film Institute and worked as a City Council advisor on media development issues. She has written about Channel 4 Television, cultural industries, the regulation of British television, and the independent film movement. Her publications include *May '68 and Film Culture* (1978); as co-editor *Television Times* (1996), *The Regions, the Nations and BBC* (1993) and *Enterprise and Heritage: Cross currents of national culture* (1991). She was one of the founders and is currently a Board member of the International Documentary Festival.

John Hunter-Jones

John Hunter-Jones is Lecturer in Leisure Management in the School of Education at The University of Manchester. Teaching areas include Leisure Law; Tourism and Economics of Leisure. He gained a BA (Hons) degree in Law from The University of Cambridge and an M.Sc in Tourism from The University of Strathclyde, but experience in commercial and public tourism preceded his first lecturing appointment in 1992. Research interests include: the development of a methodology for selecting the content for leisure law courses in higher education; Safety as an issue in the leisure sector; the role of work experience on Leisure Management degrees.

Yohji Iwamoto

Yohji Iwamoto is a Research student in the Rural History Centre/Department of Science and Technology Education, University of Reading. He was born in Nagasaki prefecture in 1963. He earned a BA in Archaeology, and an MA in Adult Education (Kyushu University, Japan), before lecturing in Education at a Japanese Higher Education College in Reading 1993-96. He is interested in the role of the private sector in post-modern society, especially its educational aspects for the environment, and is currently doing research on environmental history about the British countryside in the inter-war period.

Francis Lobo

Francis Lobo is Associate Professor in the School of Marketing Tourism and Leisure, Faculty of Business and Public Management, Edith Cowan University, Western Australia. He has been teaching and researching in the areas of leisure and sports studies for over 25 years. During the 1990s, he has researched into late career unemployment and its impact on lifestyle. He is currently examining youth unemployment and access to public provision.

Sarah McIntosh

Sarah McIntosh has been a lecturer at the Edinburgh College of Art \ Heriot Watt University for five years. She previously worked for a major economic and planning consultancy for 10 years. Her lecturing and research interests include the development process with particular regard to the interface between commercial requirements and wider socioeconomic and environmental impacts and the evaluation and appraisal of policies and projects concentrating on housing and urban regeneration initiatives.

Wilf Murphy

Wilf Murphy retired from the School of Human Sciences at John Moores University after a long career which included membership of the team responsible for the design and inauguration of the Sports Science Degree. He was specifically involved in the Sociology of Leisure and Recreation Management modules. Wilf is currently Associate Lecturer at the University of Salford in the Department of Leisure and Hospitality Studies, teaching on the BA(Hons) Leisure Management. Previously External / Advisor for a number of Leisure related courses. Wilf spent several years as Book Review Editor for the *Leisure Studies* Journal and has served as a member of the LSA Executive.

Neil Ravenscroft

Neil Ravenscroft is Reader in Leisure Management in the School of Management Studies for the Service Sector at the University of Surrey where he is responsible for developing the School's research profile. Neil has had a long term interest in leisure property and is the author of Recreation Planning and Development (Macmillan, 1992), one of the few texts to make linkages between the provision and use of leisure and recreation facilities. Neil is a current member of the LSA Executive and has been a regular contributor to LSA conferences.

Maurice Roche

Maurice Roche is Senior Lecturer, Sociology Department, Sheffield University, Sheffield, UK and is also coordinator of the SEDEC European social research network. His current research centres on the political sociology of popular culture (media, sport, tourism, and mega-events in particular) and the political sociology of citizenship (social, cultural and European in particular). His recent books on these topics are *Rethinking Citizenship: Ideology, Welfare and Change in Modern Society* (Polity Press, 1996); *Sport, Popular Culture and Identity*, (editor) (Meyer and Meyer Verlag, Aachen, 1998); *European Citizenship and Social Exclusion* (editor with Rik van Berkel) (Avebury Press, 1997). His book *Mega-Events and Modernity: Olympics, Expos and the Construction of Public Culture* (forthcoming Routledge, 1999) relates to themes in his chapter in this volume.

Martha Rowley

Martha Rowley is a graduate of Lancaster University and was, at the time the paper was written, a Research Officer at the University of Reading. She has since worked as a Research Officer for Surrey Research Group, before embarking on an eight month tour of South America. Following her under-graduate dissertation on women's use of public space, Martha has worked on a number of research contracts related to planning and the urban environment.

Fiona Simpson

Fiona Simpson graduated with a BSc (Hons) in Town Planning from Heriot Watt University \ Edinburgh College of Art in 1993. She has experience in public and private sectors of planning and recently completed doctoral research which involved a comparison of tourism capacity analysis in the Old Town of Edinburgh and the historic centre of Prague. Research interests include central and eastern Europe, historic cities and recreation and tourism planning.

John Spink

John Spink trained as a geographer and town planner in the UK and Canada. His teaching and research have focused on social scientific analysis of urban environments. His working life has been spent in West Yorkshire, both in Bradford and in Leeds, and his recent work has centred on the impact of deindustrialisation and the development of postmodern responses to urban change in northern provincial cities. Working in collaboration with Peter Bramham he has investigated leisure lifestyles of inner-city Leeds and has examined the relationships between urban policy, physical regeneration and changing leisure forms within that city.

Policy and Publics: Introduction

The relevance of 'policy' to leisure, with its cultural and commercial components, is easily discernible within the contributions to this volume. Indeed, leisure studies have deep roots in the strategic concerns of policy makers and the pragmatism of private sector leisure management. The term 'publics' — particularly in plural form — is less well established. It is employed in the title of this volume to capture the idea of public policy but one that is fragmented into dealing with diverse 'publics', traditionally acknowledged to be divided by the processes of class, gender and race. More recently, leisure researchers are tracing the symbiotic, and at times contested, relationship between public policy and consumption. Government policy generally treats the public as universal citizens, whereas commodification deals with 'taste publics', with people as consumers, targeted in niche markets.

Part One of this volume explores the nature of public culture and its history. There has been much academic and political debate during the past decade about the relative significance of the state or the market in shaping public policy. **Sylvia Harvey**'s contribution 'The Economics of Culture in a Pluralist Society' offers a welcome and articulate overview of key writings about the economy and polity of public broadcasting, in the context of leisure. Harvey revisits the concept of 'cultural industries' and the central ideas surrounding the tension between the production and consumption of cultural goods and services. The paper considers the democratic mechanisms necessary for revitalising the public sphere in face of the power of private global media corporations. Drawing on the ideas of Habermas, of public culture as free communication between equal citizens, Harvey suggests three crucial ingredients for a pluralistic democratic state: the commitment to a public broadcasting service, the need to regulate in the public interest and a determination to serve non-elite minority interests. The final section of the

1

paper grounds the debate by studying three examples from UK broadcasting — the financing of the BBC, the regulation of commercial TV and pluralism and minority interests in Channel 4 broadcasting.

The 'social construction of the public sphere' within nation states interestingly provides the cutting edge to **Maurice Roche**'s 'work-in-progress' on the vast topic of 'Mega-events and Modernity'. Cast as an exploration of the 'archeology' of post-modern culture, Roche suggests that many of the ingredients of consumer culture are to be discovered embedded in the late 19th century and the early 20th century, a period associated with the emergence of modernity. Rather than providing a history of the micro-politics of event management, the present paper focuses on the mass popularity of mega-events, in particular expositions or expos. The paper suggests that the institutional set of museums, art galleries, department stores and theme parks mediated the values of 'urban cosmopolitanism' and touristic 'consumerism', terms most closely and currently associated with the post-modern. Inspired by the work of Hobsbawm on 'invented traditions', the paper traces the cultural impact of expositions and their inter-national dimensions. Having provided a brief history of expositions 1851 to 1939 (and an extensive bibliography), Roche concludes that expos introduced a 'touristic consumer culture' with a distinctive legacy for host cities and the public culture of nation states. Read in conjunction with Harvey's paper on broadcasting, the two papers raise important questions for leisure studies about the nature and construction of public culture in modern and post-modern times.

In Part Two the consumer is again evident, both within the concern shown for public attitudes towards safety in the general leisure environment and in public participation and planning related to community development and the provision of sports stadia. Ulrich Beck's (1997)[1] characterisation of new times is one of defining social life as taking place within a 'risk society'. The lives of politicians and citizens are defined as one of risk taking in an increasing complex and problematic environment, yet safety is rarely the key element in consumer decision making. **John Hunter-Jones**' paper examines the way in which civilised society attempts to offer a safe environment for consumers. One route for leisure consumption is through safety legislation in the work place, another route is through governmental licensing of leisure activities.

The leisure sector has had to respond to substantial legislation, policed by a myriad of diverse organisations and agencies. The demands of both self regulation and free market regulation have resulted in both public legislation and also in a public prepared to resort to the civil courts to sue for breach of contract, negligence, or breach of statutory duty. The present system assumes trust by providers yet many leisure venues operate without regular inspection. As Hunter-Jones points out, deregulation can remove the freedom of the public to have safe, regulated environments.

Sports stadia have constituted one leisure site which has generated intense debate both within the media and in academic literature. The primary audience for **Sarah McIntosh and Fiona Simpson**'s contribution should be professional planners, as their research seeks to spell out good practice in relation to sports stadia and urban regeneration. They identify two major strands in the relevant literature: one concerned with policy process, the second concerned with development specific or output issues.

Drawing on a variety of case studies from England and Scotland, they suggest four categories of case study findings, labeled in the following manner: (i) local authority as a catalyst for development; (ii) viability and use profile; (iii) political and community involvement; (iv) policy implications for site selection. Eschewing the likes of Chelsea, Derby, Newcastle United and Arsenal which have been fully discussed in the media, the authors summarise the key issues underpinning diverse cases in Scotland, the North of England and the South East. They conclude with four main implications for planning sports stadia: the interaction and consistency of guidance, policy and implementation; the nature of planning; planners as mediators of stakeholder concerns; and planning and community involvement.

In Part Three, the impact of policy and provision on the public is explored. One focus is upon unemployment *per se* and its consequences on individual perceptions and leisure. In addition, an international perspective reveals how some aspects of conflict between industrial and conservation priorities might affect attitudes to developments in Japan.

If sports stadia and urban regeneration are major policy issues in the 1990s, unemployment or 'enforced leisure' was central to politicians and policy initiatives in the 1980s. **Francis Lobo**'s contribution provides a welcome reminder of the impact of job loss on people's lives and suggests that the positive use of leisure depends upon the intensity of job loss impact. After summarising two major perspectives on the psychology of unemployment — deprivation and personal agency approaches, Lobo briefly maps out the concepts of 'serious' leisure and leisure capital to provide the context for interpreting the three case studies of the differential impact of the experience of job loss. Drawing from a wider study, his research methodology focused on in-depth interviews with three unemployed males, their spouses and one family offspring respectively. These interviews were completed on three separate occasions over a year to map out the impact of job loss. Pen pictures follow of the differential impact of job loss in the lives of these individuals and the study concludes with the hope that "providers using leisure programmes to ameliorate the deprivations of unemployment take the impact of job loss into account when participants are accepted into schemes for the unemployed".

Yohji Iwamoto's paper is concerned with the links, real and potential, between industry, commerce, conservationism and leisure provision within the concept of green tourism. He allocates a considerable amount of time to setting the scene. Both historical development and the current situation are described, highlighting the influence of various government agencies and the interaction of commercialism and traditional sociocultural values. Evidence of research activity is presented with a certain scepticism regarding the value of adopting cross-cultural models for analysis. Final discussion is concerned with the survival of rural, agricultural tourist areas and implies significant political and economic undertones. It also reports the interesting advice given by financial experts to a typical household (i.e. to cut leisure expenditure by half) as well as accurately forecasting a downturn in the Japanese economy.

Part Four analyses two aspects of city centre culture related to the physical (property) resources available and the planned provision and promotion of a preconceived image. Again, concern is with policies and people together with urban change and regeneration. The papers in this section therefore complement each other very well.

The growth of retail centres and the advent of leisure shopping, together with various related political, social and cultural aspects of development, has been the subject of much discussion and debate in recent years. **Sarah Rowley and Neil Ravenscroft** indicate how continued concern has been manifest in the interest shown by politicians, British and European, and has resulted in the production of guidelines for development in these areas. Development has had a great deal of impact on some town centres and the property they contain. They focus, therefore, on the "Social and cultural outcome of the changing physical structure of town centres and the impact this has on those using (or excluded from) these spaces", and also question the extent to which the development of leisure businesses contributes to the vitality and viability of town centres.

In the case of Reading, data utilised relate to "property occupation and values, pedestrian flows and public attitudes to usage of the town centre, supplemented by evidence about leisure property". Rowley and Ravenscroft believe that there is no strong evidence, at the moment, that investors will shift their interest from edge-of-town site back to town centres, where leisure properties will continue to be smaller and developed as a result of 'opportunism'. Town centre managers, it is suggested, also engage in opportunism whilst promoting their versions of the 'post-modern city'. Paradoxically, however, the characteristics displayed in this opportunistic leisure development — that is, lack of permanence and a necessary flexibility, together with perceived lack of safety — render some city centres vulnerable and susceptible to "eventual replacement by sanitised, policed leisure parks".

The final paper deals with leisure and city centre development, focusing on the 24-hour/living city scenario, using Leeds as the exemplar and main sources of debate. **John Spink and Peter Bramham** have produced a well-structured paper which permits informed deliberation without requiring intimate knowledge of the city in question, using policy formulation, implementation and evaluation as the model to assist analysis. The policy and planning section describes the "living city" concept of integration — that is, working, shopping, leisure and residence to counter a nine-to-five urban pattern. The policy adopted by Leeds authorities, based on their interpretation of the 'new socialist political philosophy', is clearly demonstrated.

The second section of the paper focuses on deregulation and promotion. It highlights the influence of the 'Manchester model' on decision making, whilst changes of attitude to city centre development — from an "old municipal Labour puritan regulation approach, to one of enabler" — are also outlined. Despite delineation of some specific examples of development in this area of provision, doubt and scepticism about the inclusivity of the initiatives seem to pervade the authors' opinions.

The reality of the transformed and regenerated city centre situation is spelled out in section three of the paper. The search for 24-hour status involves large investment in management and surveillance. Current results, however, indicate a predominant downtown, night-time youth culture where segregation by age, gender and ethnicity with young male domination has tended to promote the 'boys zone' image, rather than the "living city" intentions of civic authorities and planners.

Conference papers are notoriously eclectic and at various stages of development. Nevertheless, the papers selected for inclusion in this volume [authors presented their original versions at the LSA's September 1997 conference hosted by Roehampton Institute London] provide testimony to the interest that leisure researchers share in exploring the shifting boundaries between public policy, provision and patterns of consumption. Leisure therefore provides an interesting, and often neglected, site for the exploration of changes in policy, provision and participation.

Peter Bramham
Leeds Metropolitan University

Wilf Murphy
The University of Salford

Note

1   Beck, Ulrich (1997) 'Risk Society', in Franklin, J. (ed) *The Politics of a Risk Society*. Cambridge: Polity Press.

I

Public Culture in Modernity

The Economics of Culture in a Pluralistic Society

Sylvia Harvey

Sheffield Hallam University

Introduction

In the world of confusion and uncertainty that replaces the certain controversies of the Cold War we have to re-examine our understanding of the processes whereby human beings fashion themselves, either through the activities of their free time or through their actions performed in 'unfree time' in the world of work. I shall concentrate here on the fashioning of the social self that takes place within leisure time. And since, in the electrified western world, people spend what is probably the largest single component of their leisure time in front of the television set I shall explore some of the determinants at work in the construction of broadcasting systems. For it is these systems that produce many of the emotional and cognitive materials that we, as individual human agents, take up and weave into our sense of self and of other and that contribute to our understanding of the state of the world and our place within it.

My purpose is to reflect upon the role that broadcasting might play in making and maintaining a pluralistic culture as we enter the new millennium, suggesting that it is the economics of culture, at least as much as the politics of pluralism, that will determine the outcome of this project. This discussion involves, predictably, some arguments about method and emphasis in the analysis of leisure and culture and, in particular, revolves around the issue of the role of the market and of public regulation in determining levels and types of cultural provision (Peacock, 1986; Blumler and Nossiter, 1991; Congdon, 1992; Graham and Davies, 1997).

The fall of the Berlin Wall has come to signal the emergence of a new age of opportunity and of anxiety. And the dissipation of Cold War beliefs and energies has resulted in some questioning of the old antinomies of market and state provision or, more exactly, a recognition that there are advantages

9

and limitations to both types of provision (Hutton, 1996; Kelly, *et al.*, 1997). The old command economies of the socialist states have seemed to be productively inadequate, whether in the production of fridges or television programmes, and state or party control of all areas of social and cultural life has been seen to place unacceptable limits on personal freedom. And yet the very questioning of communist practice and its apparent yielding to a newly victorious capitalist model has also thrown into sharp relief some of the limitations of the free market model.

The former Soviet Union and the previously iron-curtained countries of central and eastern Europe have sought to learn the lessons of the capitalist market and to enter the capitalist club, but in the process they and their erstwhile antagonists have had to confront cultural as well as economic issues. In the world of broadcasting, particularly in advertiser-funded systems, the messages from the consumer 'frontline', that is from television ratings, have come increasingly to dominate decisions about what programmes are to be made and transmitted. While some knowledge of and sensitivity to audience choice is vital for the development of a democratic broadcasting system, and the development of 'add-on' specialist subscription services may extend consumer choice, the dangers of too heavy a reliance upon ratings information are also well-known. A ratings-driven system may concede too much power to advertisers and their views about which audiences matter; it may result in blandness and a fear of offending any powerful interests in the content of programmes, and it may severely curtail the creative freedom of the people who make the programmes.

Together, these dangers put at risk the project of cultural pluralism and of freedom of expression. Moreover the most cursory inspection of a free market in mass-produced culture demonstrates both the tendency to monopoly and a deference to the socially and economically powerful which declines to serve unpopular, critical or non-elite minority interests. The social historian Harold Perkin has suggested that particular business interests have advanced arguments about the value of competition in a free market in order to distract attention from an actual tendency to monopoly:

> The ideology of the free market appeals to the professional managers of great corporations and their allies because it protects them from the accusation they most fear, that they themselves are the major threat to competition and the freedom of the citizen. By denying the incontrovertible fact that competition drives out competitors and tends towards monopoly, it enables them to present themselves as the guardians of the consumer and the deliverers of the widest choice of goods and services at the lowest prices. (Perkin, 1989: pp. 12-13)

In noting the claim of the great corporation to be the defender of consumer interests, Perkin also emphasises the specifically political nature of arguments linking the idea of free choice in the market to the idea of political freedom (or even to the proposition that the free market is the only guarantor of political freedom). It is this second connection between market freedom and political freedom that has allowed the large private corporations to 'claim to be the guardians of individual liberty against the tyranny of the state' (Perkin, 1989: p. 13). And it is this second argument that has had such powerful resonance in the societies of Russia, eastern and central Europe seeking a speedy resolution to the problem of too much state power.

But there is an irony here for those societies struggling to diminish the power of the state, since in mature capitalist societies the state has been used to disposing of between 40% and 60% of gross domestic product (Perkin, 1989: p. 10). We can see from this that the passionate defence of the free market, while it represents an ideal for some, is something of an anachronism when it comes to accurate description of the contemporary world. None-theless, as a mechanism, the market can provide useful information as to consumer demand and, in many cases, an efficient means for allocating resources. I shall argue here that while, in the case of cultural provision, the market can be a useful indicator of preference it is ultimately an inadequate mechanism for maintaining the kind of cultural pluralism that can be regarded as a key characteristic of the democratic state.

Leisure studies and the role of the market

Like all respectable disciplines in the late twentieth century Leisure Studies has its own share of number-crunchers and idealists, philosophers and theorists. Moreover, the entropic messages of post-modernism, for those who have come under their spell, have encouraged thinkers in this field as in many others to live happily with fragmentation, separation and disasso-ciation, banishing the issues of universality, totality and causality from the realms of academic discourse. The impulse to fragment and to relativise has come from many different directions, some of it driven by what Raymond Williams would have called the new realism of subordinated groups claiming a voice and the right to develop their own forms of cultural expression. Many such groups have challenged previously dominant ways of seeing the world including (as an example from the field of leisure) gender-biased definitions of the concept of 'free time'.

That these particular and necessary challenges to the taken-for-granted assumptions of an old order should have been burdened with the label of 'political correctness' on the one hand, and the remit of the post-modern mission to fragment on the other is, in my view, unfortunate and intellectually unproductive. In this paper I want to reclaim something of the pre-post-modern vision of structure, relationship, cause and connectedness in exploring a different set of claims to correctness: those involving the nature of the relationship between economy and society, economic imperatives and cultural forms. If this sounds like a return to the old marxist proposition of 'base' determining 'superstructure' (perhaps the strongest form of connection that you can get) this may be no bad thing.

However, there are some key differences this time around. Our recent recovery of a kind of economic determinism (or at least a sense of economic primacy) has been noticeable since the 1980s in studies of the 'cultural industries' and of the 'economic case for the arts' (Greater London Ccuncil, 1985; Mulgan and Worpole, 1986; Myerscough, 1988; Harvey, 1988; Lewis, 1990). But this has grown out of a complex interweaving of previously distinct political philosophies and positions, and sometimes these studies grew out of a desire on the part of those in opposition to achieve some of their ends by adopting the language of those in power. This complicated historical dynamic, not quite reducible to the manic bricolage of distressed minds, has lead us in the 1990s towards new territory, to a political space described by Anthony Giddens as 'beyond left and right' (Giddens, 1994).

Something of the confusing migration and multivalence of positions becomes apparent as we note that, in the Thatcher-Reagan era, it was the free marketeers of the radical right who argued that the economy plays a crucial role in determining people's sense of themselves and behaviour in the world: create a plethora of small businesses and a casualised labour market and the values of the enterprise culture will follow (Corner and Harvey, 1991: pp. 1-20). The irony is that such ideas emerged in the wake of widespread attempts within western marxism to minimise the role of economic causality and to emphasise, rather, the relative autonomy of superstructure from base. An intellectual eclecticism to-day, rising from the ranks of the free market right or the social democratic left, might emphasise rather the double-directional pull of causalities: the economy acts upon culture but culture also acts upon the economy.

This paper argues, in concert with a long tradition of cultural materialist thinking, that the life of cultural forms — the 'breath of the spirit' as it were — depends upon a skeleton or infrastructure of economic activities and relationships. Furthermore, and in the light of an attachment to the interventionism of public policy-making and implementation, I shall argue that the emergence and maintenance of a pluralistic society, involving the complex democratic project of inclusion, equality and difference, depends upon 'getting right' a set of economic activities in the field of culture. This is not the same as the argument that only an unfettered market can establish appropriate or 'correct' levels of cultural provision.

The language of correctness has become a commonplace of capitalist economic theory, attributing to the market a high degree of precision in providing information and consequent systemic intelligence in managing economic activity. Moreover the advocacy of market mechanisms has taken on a whole new lease of life in the light of the sometimes disastrous failures of the political command economy within socialist or communist states. There are, however, some equally familiar difficulties involved in viewing the market as sole and sufficient indicator of consumer preference. There may be consumers who cannot afford, but who nonetheless need, a particular commodity (this might be true of housing or of healthcare), and in the realm of cultural expression and leisure provision there may be particular forms and services which the free market cannot sustain but which 'civilised society' arguments defend as in some way necessary. At a general level such arguments have resulted in the provision of public finance for a variety of services and institutions from heart by-pass operations to live theatre, from art galleries to public service broadcasting. Thus the state intervenes in order to provide services which the market alone cannot provide, enabled not by private capital but by the mechanisms of tax collection.

These arguments and counter-arguments are inevitably present within the fields of leisure and cultural studies. But while market activity is often seen as a natural process ('leave it to the market'), state activity is sometimes seen to be disruptively interventionist, disturbing the proper circulation of commodities in the free market. The market argument was put with some force by an early contributor to the journal *Leisure Studies*, R. W. Vickerman, who noted "...the well-known difficulty...that in the absence of a market there is no test of the correctness of the level of provision". However, in terms of familiar social democratic and patrician conservative arguments about a possible interventionist role for the state, he also and immediately notes an exception:

> ... except ultimately through the ballot box, where it is often very difficult to identify separately issues such as the level of provision of individual services. (Vickerman, 1983: p. 358)

It is the 'market test' view and its associated objective of creating a market in broadcasting services which motivated the work of the Peacock Committee, invited by the British government in 1985 to examine methods of financing the British Broadcasting Corporation. I shall return later to some of the still live issues raised by the report of this Committee (Peacock, 1986).

Since 1989 the role and status of the free market has been subjected to critical scrutiny from many directions, and the questioning of old borders and beliefs has resulted in some new and unexpected intellectual and political configurations. Monroe Price in his account of media transformations in the post-communist world offers an intriguing account of a seminar held in Washington in 1992 under the auspices of the American Enterprise Institute. At this event, he suggests, the participants:

> ... exhibited an anguished consciousness and substantial discomfiture over the impact of American programming — broadly conceived — on the flowering of democracy in the post-Communist transition societies. (Price, 1995: p. 21)

He points out that the note of caution regarding an international free market in culture was voiced "not by European Marxists but by a group of American neo-conservatives":

> Many of the panellists were concerned that filling the foreign public space with Wheel of Fortune and the throbbing and distracting siren songs of MTV might subvert or inhibit the building of democratic practices...An overly zealous commercial culture, they worried, would pre-empt the development of an adequately functional political culture. (Price, 1995: p. 22)

I shall return later to the issue of creating an 'adequately functional political culture' in exploring the concepts of civil society and the public sphere in relationship to the cultural role of broadcasting. But at this point it may be useful to situate some of the assumptions of the enterprise culture within a broader history.

Capitalist theory has consistently argued that the free market is the best and most efficient allocative mechanism, thus capitalist markets have established demand and set prices, ensuring the brisk circulation of commodities and the most efficient use of labour and raw materials, given the available technologies of production. The Russian Revolution of 1917 tried to change all that, announcing the creation of a workers' state and the removal of a capitalist class, introducing the principle of social not private ownership of the means of production, and attempting to gear a whole economic system, under the direct command of the workers' state, to the meeting of human need not the making of profit.

Western capitalist states, responding to the political challenge of this then radical Soviet utopianism, as well as to the pressure of their own workers' movements, moved to create a hybrid form of capitalism: the welfare state. Within these states, to a greater or lesser extent, the allocative mechanisms of the market were undermined or complemented by forms of public provision in the areas of health, education, housing and culture. Throughout the period of universal suffrage in capitalist democracies (from the 1920s) the arguments about 'freeing the market' or 'enabling the state' have ebbed and flowed according to circumstances (the stock market crash of 1929, the World War of 1939-45) and the electoral strength of the different political parties.

Despite the obvious inadequacies of such a thumbnail sketch it is important to locate debates about cultural production and leisure provision within this broader framework of the vicissitudes of the free market ideal. In Britain in the 1980s the political priorities of Prime Minister Margaret Thatcher gave a tremendous boost to free market ideas, emphasising individual initiative, business enterprise and the privatisation of state-held assets in areas as diverse as air travel, telecommunications, gas, water and electricity. In the world of the arts many were shocked by the views of a Conservative minister who declared that people would only value what they paid for. In the field of broadcasting licences were to be allocated to the highest bidder and the Prime Minister herself took the view that there was "no such thing as society, only individuals and their families". A wide range of activities were scrutinised, justified or condemned almost exclusively in terms of their viability within the market, although by the end of the decade different voices were raising questions about the wisdom of such an approach. Anthony Smith, for example, in a paper prepared for the Arts Council suggested that:

> The arts can restore something of what we have lost in the transition from citizens to consumers, from souls to purses .... They can transform our sense of what is real. (Smith, 1993: p. 124)

Since the subsidised arts and public service broadcasting relied for their existence upon a notion of social and cultural service and values, the tougher dictates of the enterprise culture came to be feared. There seemed not to be a public language for the discussion of values other than those of the balance sheet. And this gave rise to a new kind of public rhetoric about the economic importance of the arts and cultural industries, since this seemed to be the only basis on which their future might be secured. It is not my intention here to argue that balance sheets do not matter, clearly they do. And it is useful for any economic development strategy to be aware of the potential for job creation within a range of cultural activities, of the export potential of particular cultural products and so forth. But assessments of market viability in themselves do not ensure the presence of a rich and pluralistic culture, nor that the less popular cultural forms remain publicly available, nor that the interests of non-elite minorities will be met.

Re-viewing the 'cultural industries'

In 1958 Raymond Williams argued that the study of culture involved an understanding of the relations between elements in 'a whole way of life'. He thereby drew the infant discipline of cultural studies into the wake of anthropological accounts of all aspects of cultural activity and expression including the study of pre-capitalist forms (Williams, 1966: p. 12). His broad approach to the study of contemporary culture included an interest in both commodity and non-commodity forms. However, it is the sub-set 'culture-as-commodity' that most concerns us here, where the term 'commodity' is taken to refer to those cultural artefacts, services or rights that can be traded in a market. Of course, forms of cultural expression: preaching, singing, dancing, making music, painting pictures and telling stories existed long before their commodification. And part of the richness and complexity of culture within contemporary capitalist societies stems from the fact that it continues to exist in non-commodity as well as in commodity form. Every human being who uses their voice box to tell a joke or hum a tune is involved in cultural production of a non-commodity kind, though they will probably have another existence as cultural consumers who pay to listen to other people's jokes, other people's music and other people's stories.

In the twentieth century large industries have developed to produce and sell cultural goods and services, and it has become a key characteristic of richer societies that 'leisure spending' (which includes cultural spending) continues to rise as a proportion of total consumer spending. In 1996 leisure spending in Britain was estimated to represent just over a quarter of all consumer spending and to be worth £129 billion (Leisure Consultants, 1997: p. 58). However, since the emphasis of this paper is on television it is important to note that while television viewing represents a large share of the use of 'free time' — around 50% — it constitutes a rather small share of total leisure spending — under 10% (British Film Institute, 1996: p. 46; Advertising Association, 1996: p. 96). In addition, although people in Britain may spend a great deal of their spare time at home, it has been estimated that over 70% of their leisure spending occurs away from home; and the forecasts are that this will increase relative to home-based spending (Leisure Consultants, 1997: p. 58). So, in various ways, there is a clear 'mismatch' between where most money is spent and where most time is spent.

Before examining the provenance and use of the term 'cultural industries' it may be useful to offer a brief sketch of the vital statistics of the audio-visual sector in Britain. Cinema is the least significant economically, although it continues to have considerable cultural impact through the medium of video as well as on terrestrial, cable and satellite television. Cinema attendances have been rising steadily since 1984 though they still represent only a fraction of the numbers achieved in the 'golden age' before television. In 1995 admissions had climbed to just over 114 million a year which gives an average of around two visits a year per person; the average figure for 1946 was 34 visits a year (BFI, 1996: p. 33; BFI, 1993: p. 34). It is also worth noting, in terms of international comparisons, that while cinema-going in Britain is close to the European average the activity is now more than twice as popular in the United States with an average in 1993 of 4.8 visits per head per year (BFI, 1994: p. 34).

We should also compare the amount of time and money spent at the cinema and watching television in Britain. If we estimate that an average of two visits to the cinema per year represents about five hours of time spent before the large screen, this contrasts with annual, average television viewing figure of over 1,200 hours (BFI, 1996: p. 33, 46). The differences of scale are remarkable. In terms of economic value we can also compare the relative worth of cinema, video, satellite movie channels and terrestrial television. The figures for 1995, expressed in billions of pounds, are as follows:

Value of the British Audio-Visual sector in 1995

	£billion	Percentage Value
Cinema Box Office:	0.38	6%
Movie Channel Subscriptions:	0.70	11%
Video Sales and Rental:	1.20	20%
Terrestrial Television:	3.90	63%

(BFI, 1997: pp. 33, 28, 33, 50; BBC, 1996: p. 4)

This is a snapshot of a rapidly changing market and while it seems likely that video sales may now have peaked, movie subscriptions will probably continue to increase. We could summarise the present state of affairs by noting that movie subscriptions are already worth nearly twice the value of cinema box office and that video sales and rentals represent rather more that three times the value of box office. While terrestrial television is worth ten times the value of cinema (1). These figures seem to emphasise the relative significance of a home base for the enjoyment of audio-visual pleasures. Although, of course, people do not necessarily spend most time (or even most money) on what matters to them most, and the pleasure of a night out at the cinema might be remembered long after the memory of hundreds of hours of television viewing had faded.

As leisure spending increases, investors are increasingly looking for ways of tapping into this market, of inventing new commodities and competing for consumers across the range of older and newer forms of leisure and cultural provision. Forecasts produced within the field of leisure studies help to place television within a much broader context of changing patters of expenditure and also help to give us a relative sense of the economic importance of home-based leisure activities as against other forms of leisure expenditure. So, for example, one set of estimates for leisure spending in Britain in 1996 rank 'home entertainment' as the fourth largest category (at 10.4% of the total) easily out-ranked by the 'top three' of alcoholic drink (21.3%), eating out (19.3%) and holidays overseas (14.4%) (Leisure Consultants, 1997: p. 58).

In general terms the audio-visual figures given above significantly understate the economic value of satellite television in Britain. The usefulness of the comparison between cinema box office and movie channel subscriptions leaves out of account the additional revenue generated by one of the most popular forms of subscription television namely, sports. Some recently published figures for 1997 indicate a Sky Sports subscriber base of 6.4 million and a new monthly charge, for 3 sports channels, of £24.99 (Varley, 1997: p. 3). This would be likely to generate in 1998 a sum of around £1.9 billion. Interestingly this is almost exactly the same amount as the total value of the BBC licence fee for 1997 (BBC, 1997: p. 5). The licence fee, by contrast, resources a highly diverse output across two national television channels, five national radio channels and 38 local radio stations. Moreover the production costs incurred by Sky Sports and by the BBC are very different. A clear majority of BBC peak-time television programmes (73%) are original, not repeats, and they are made in Britain (BBC, 1997: p. 18). And some of this material for example drama, at a per hour cost of £468, 000, or documentaries, at an hourly cost of £124, 000, is considerably more expensive to produce than sports programmes; for sports the BBC's own figure is £70, 000 per hour (BBC, 1997: p. 94). I shall return to some of the questions of value for money and cultural value in the last section of this paper.

Another way of interpreting the audio-visual figures for Britain would be to note that television seems to represent a remarkably cost-effective way of providing large amounts of information and entertainment. Furthermore the BBC has argued that public service broadcasting is the most cost-effective form of all, publishing figures which claimed that while the 1996 cost per hour of viewing and listening to BBC services was four pence, the cost of a typical satellite subscription package was eighteen pence per hour and the cost of video hire 57 pence per hour (BBC, 1997: p. 94).

These are the statistics that tell us about time and money, but what is their cultural significance? What additional or alternative values might be attributed to the figures outlined above? Probably the first thing to

acknowledge is that in cultural studies we still have a very limited understanding of the meaning-making chain. And we tend now to be much more
cautious than an earlier generation of critics of mass communication who
tended to attribute both significance and social effect (usually of a negative
kind) to particular media texts, with very little empirical evidence to support
their theses. The term 'cultural industries' makes only a limited contribution
to our assessment of the particular meaning and impact of cultural forms.
However, it can help us to address the mapping question raised by Williams
concerning the 'relations between elements in a whole way of life'. since
industrialised cultural production — production on a large scale — is now
such an important feature of the meaning-making processes in our society.
These industries of music, cinema, press and broadcasting provide us, as
I suggested earlier, with so many of the materials which we use to identify
ourselves and to locate ourselves as social beings.

The term 'culture industry' or cultural industries emerged in the mid-
twentieth century as cultural analysts sought to account for the emergence
of industrialised and commodified culture. Theodor Adorno and Max Horkheimer claimed to be the first to use the term in their book *Dialectic of
Enlightenment*, published in 1947 (Adorno, 1991: p. 85). A number of
different definitions of the 'cultural industries' are available, and the term
has been inflected in a number of different directions in accordance with the
objectives of different and sometimes opposed political ideologies. A minimal
definition would be that these industries involve the multiple reproduction
of cultural goods, produced by technological means and available in commodity form (Harvey, 1988: p. Interim Report, 9). The use of the adjective
'cultural' indicates that these goods have symbolic properties, that they
involve human meaning-making.

Since the 1980s and in the case of urban regeneration strategies (often
also involving a tourism component) the term has been used by public
authorities, planners and cultural consultants in a very general way to
embrace a wide range of activities from visual art to craft, from cinema
exhibition to sports facilities. Such usage has its own pragmatic justifications
but rather obscures the specific and modern nature of these industries. The
definition offered previously has, arguably, some quite usefully exclusive
elements. The cultural industries, in this sense, do not include small scale
craft forms of production, nor the pre-industrial forms of live music and
theatrical performance, since what is live is not recorded or multiply reproduced; the live event is unique. Nor do they include painting and sculpture,
unless mechanically or electronically reproduced, nor leisure activities such
as swimming which, arguably, lack a specifically symbolic dimension (though,
of course, as activities they exist within complex chains of social meaning
and value). One final aspect of these industries may be worth noting here.
It has been argued that they operate as an integrated economic whole since
they compete for a limited amount of consumption time and disposable
income, and draw upon a limited pool of advertising finance and skilled
labour (Garnham, 1990: p. 158).

To advocate the use of a restricted definition of cultural industries — one which excludes the live and fine arts — is not to suggest that these pre-industrial forms lack importance or value. Indeed the opposite may be the case; they may become even more valuable — in a cultural not economic sense — in a society dominated by mass reproduction. For the great economies of scale which are possible within the cultural industries, and the fact that their 'prototypes' (the films, television dramas, news items) are expensive to produce, whereas the costs of their reproduction are marginal, mean that these industries are both most oriented towards the market, most suitable for economic exploitation and potentially highly profitable. The key to their profitability is distribution and it is control or dominance in this area that both builds markets and betokens the tendency to monopoly.

Predictably there have been various attempts to use the power of the state and of the public purse to limit these monopoly tendencies and to provide a wider variety of cultural experiences and products than the market alone might sustain. Some of the most detailed work in this field was undertaken by the famously anti-Thatcherite Greater London Council (GLC) in the early 1980s. In their analysis of the cultural industries they note:

> It is clear that control of distribution, of the route to the audience, is the key site of power in the cultural industries...around distribution and channels of access to audiences we find the highest levels of capital concentration. (GLC, 1985: p. 177, 178)

However, in addition to advocating public investment initiatives in distribution (for example in music), the GLC study also points out that the public sector itself already has considerable distribution resources in the form of public broadcasting and the public library system.

The economic strength of the privately owned cultural industries may also be seen as one of their weaknesses since the temptation is always there to drive out the disturbing, the innovative and the minority interest item, should these impede profitability and the creation of a political environment which supports this goal. These objectives of profitability (and their associated political or public relations projects) can cut across the demands of cultural pluralism, that is, of the need to provide cultural resources, and a voice, for a wide variety of types of people.

Since the 1930s both conservative and anti-capitalist critics of the mass media have dismissed the media and their users, seeing in the cinema, radio and popular publishing nothing but forms of cheap and trivialising entertainment lacking all the vigorous and incisive characteristics of the work of art. It is perhaps as a result of this chequered history of critique that most western capitalist societies have acknowledged the importance of a continuing non-commodity role for certain forms of cultural production — often designated by the term 'art' — and have provided forms of public subsidy for them. These are the forms of cultural expression which would have difficulty surviving in a free market and they are predominantly the pre-industrial forms. However as we shall see — and particularly in the field of broadcasting

— the alternative mechanism of regulation may be as significant an instrument for fostering cultural pluralism as the mechanism of arts subsidy.

Writers like Adorno and Horkheimer were strongly influenced by the marxist critique of capitalist society and barely able to emerge from the deep anguish caused by first-hand experience of German fascism and the shock of enforced migration to the America of 'Hollywood the dream factory'. It is perhaps unsurprising, therefore, that their use of the term 'culture industry' is almost wholly critical and evaluative, not merely descriptive. For them this industry, maker of mass culture, represents 'mass deception', the decay of reason, the triumph of the superficial and the standardised and the pursuit of profit to the exclusion of any human or aesthetic concerns (Adorno and Horkheimer, 1977). The 'consciousness industry' eliminates the 'autonomy of works of art' and produces in American society what later critics came to call the 'air-conditioned nightmare' or what Herbert Marcuse referred to as the society of 'one dimensional man' (Marcuse, 1964). This at once diminished and spectacular culture is seen to represent a closing down of the universe of rational discourse, a terrifying slamming shut of the gates against reason and the critical faculties.

Contemporary cultural studies has moved away from this hostile critique of the cultural industries in at least three ways. It has celebrated the popular in popular culture, validating the pleasures entailed in cultural consumption. It has rejected the conservative critique as rooted in a set of aesthetic and other values not shared by all. And it has argued that audiences far from being passive receivers, actively process and even transform the significance of what they consume. We could summarise this position in the rather superficial language of the late 1990s by saying that the so-called 'dumbing-down' of the media cannot have adverse effects upon an audience who are not themselves dumb.

However, this defence of the audience as both pleasure-seeker and critic fails to offer us any purchase on the activities of cultural production. In taking the cultural industries as a given these views can, while appearing radical, in practice reinforce a quite complacent attitude to the cultural status quo. In concentrating on that moment in the meaning-making chain which is the encounter between 'reader' and 'text' this position can obscure questions about production resources — the moment of production in the meaning-making chain — avoiding issues raised by a study of the economics of culture and of other institutional and regulatory determinants upon cultural production. In the last section of this paper I shall try to link the issue of resources and of the various determinants upon cultural production to the idea of the public sphere as developed by Jurgen Habermas and others.

Broadcasting, pluralism and the public sphere

For the advocates of the free market who claim their inspiration from Adam Smith the two great antagonists of the twentieth century are the state and the market. Moreover, these thinkers have no doubt that the market must be encouraged to vanquish or at least to limit the power of the state. However, in the course of a process of maturing political opposition to the communist state within eastern central Europe, a third term: 'civil society' has re-emerged and invited us to re-think the significance of this great battle between state and market. In the communist 'east' it was a wide range of clubs and voluntary associations, quite outwith the control of the state, that provided within the seed bed of civil society an opposition that finally destroyed that state. (Keane, 1984 and 1988; Cohen and Arato, 1994). There is much to reflect on here from the point of view of political theory and practice, but we must focus, in a much more limited way, on the significance of the term for an understanding of culture and communication. Cohen and Arato offer a useful definition:

> We understand 'civil society' as a sphere of social interaction between economy and state, composed above all of the intimate sphere (especially the family), the sphere of associations (especially voluntary associations), social movements, and forms of public communication. (Cohen and Arato, 1994: p. ix)

What characterises this civil society is a high degree of pluralism as well as a measure of independence from both state and market. Moreover, as Cohen and Arato suggest, one of its key elements is 'public communication' vital for the creation of a well-informed political culture. Indeed the creation of institutions that facilitate public communication becomes a key goal for democratic societies seeking to encourage participation, sustain pluralism and avoid the dangers of a 'tyranny of the majority'. It is some of these issues that Monroe Price alludes to in the terms of 'an adequately functional political culture' in his study of the changes in broadcasting policy and practice in Russia and eastern Europe. So it may be appropriate now to turn to a brief consideration of the idea of the 'public sphere' conceived of as one of the means for fostering public communication.

Some thirty years before the velvet and other revolutions of 1989, Jurgen Habermas had developed an extensive and historically-rooted theory of the public sphere considering both its emergence as part of the early history of bourgeois society and (from his point-of-view) its subsequent decline and decay as a consequence of the widespread commodification of culture. He traces the slow process of the emergence of public opinion out of the crucible of the Enlightenment and in contradistinction to the practices of the auto-cratic monarchical state. He cites one account offered in the 1770s by a pre-revolutionary French thinker; public opinion is:

> ... an invisible power that, without treasury, without bodyguard, without army, lays down laws — laws obeyed even in the palace of the king. (Habermas, 1989: p. 263)

Across the channel Edmund Burke, sceptic and critic of revolutionary practice, offered a similarly positive endorsement of the role of public opinion seeing in it a power that rendered valid the work of government:

> ... no other given part of legislative right can be exercised without regard to the general opinion of those who are to be governed. That general opinion is the vehicle and organ of legislative omnipotence. (Habermas, 1989: p. 94)

For Habermas the public sphere, rising out of the coffee shops of eighteenth century London and the clubs and associations of revolutionary France, has certain key characteristics. It facilitates the formation of public opinion through the free exchange of information and ideas among citizens who enter that sphere on equal terms:

> By 'the public sphere' we mean first of all a realm of our social life in which something approaching public opinion can be formed. Access is guaranteed to all citizens. (Habermas, 1979: p. 198)

In the twentieth century this public sphere has been constituted through the media of mass communication. But Habermas sees in the process of industrialisation and commodification a diminishing of the power and validity of this sphere. Through a process of 're-feudalisation' the large corporations establish their own interests and limit the power of the state to act as a representative of the public interest. Thus in the period of the welfare state the public sphere is 'characterised by a peculiar weakening of its critical functions' (Habermas, 1979: p. 200). It becomes a space for the promotion of elite private interests as rational debate gives way to the spectacular world of sentiment and public relations. Monroe Price re-states this concern in his recent study of changes in American and Russian broadcasting:

> Television, as it evolves in the 'free market', does not necessarily contribute to, and often detracts from, a public forum in which citizens have equitable access, where wealth and power diminish as requisites for entry, and where opinions can be formed that serve as a check and influence on the activities of the state. (Price, 1995: p. 245)

Habermas' rather pessimistic account of the rise and fall of the public sphere was first developed in Germany in the early 1960s at a time when, as he later notes, television had barely established itself. More recently, as the chief perceived source of threat to egalitarian culture has shifted from the agents of social democracy to the proponents of the free market, and as Habermas has noted the probably positive effects of secondary education in promoting more critical attitudes to mass communication, his work has reflected a slightly more optimistic view of the potential of public communication. In rejecting as overly simplistic his earlier diagnosis of an absolute decline from a 'culture-debating to a culture-consuming public', he has recognised the potential of a 'resisting power' and of the 'critical potential of a pluralistic, internally much differentiated mass public' (Habermas, 1993: p. 438). It is this more positive view of the potential for generating debate and criticism within the public sphere, and of mobilising broadcasting as an agent of this process, that shapes the general approach of this paper.

I turn, in conclusion, to a brief examination of three examples of actually existing broadcasting organisation and regulation within Britain. It seems to me that these instances of current practice embody some of the key elements required for building and renewing a lively and critical public sphere, conceived of as the basis for the development of a democratic state.

In terms of the great audio-visual pleasures of our time I have already indicated something of the economic scale of broadcasting and of the large amount of leisure time which it occupies. I also suggested, in an earlier part of the paper, that public support and subsidy for the pre-industrial arts should be regarded as an important component of cultural pluralism and therefore of cultural democracy. But I shall concentrate here on the three features of broadcasting in Britain which seem to me to provide in embryo, the necessary conditions for a re-vitalised public sphere. These features are: a commitment to the principle of broadcasting as a public service, a recognition of the need for regulation in the public interest (including the existence of legal requirements for impartiality) and a determination to serve non-elite minority interests in the field of cultural expression.

(i) Public Service Broadcasting: the example of the BBC

The current method of financing the British Broadcasting Corporation as a public service seems to me to be one of the best available examples of an economic infrastructure designed to sustain cultural objectives. Although the licence fee is a kind of poll tax (unlike income tax it is not differentially levied according to personal wealth), it nonetheless provides a crucial means of independence from direct financing by government. Moreover this economic base provides the necessary (though not sufficient) condition for BBC accountability to its various audiences who, collectively, meet the costs of programme production. The 'old' BBC had a lofty sense of purpose often rather disconnected from any detailed research into or understanding of audience interests. However, one of the consequences of the Thatcherite onslaught on the supposedly wasteful, inward-looking and elitist BBC has been the preparation of mission statements more detailed and more pluralistic than anything produced in the past. In a 1992 document the Corporation outlined the following four objectives:

> To ensure that issues of importance to the nation, irrespective of immediate commercial popular appeal, will be properly reported, debated and analysed.

> To provide universal access ... to the broadest range of issues, voices and styles.

> To be an active cultural patron...originating and commissioning new works and developing excellence in the arts.

> To portray a multiracial, multicultural society and to respond to the diversity of cultures within the U.K. (BBC, 1992: p. 20, 22)

Taken together these objectives offer a good working definition of what one might expect to find in a properly functioning public sphere; although institutional practice and programme output, as opposed to policy statements, would need to be carefully monitored. This would be especially important as regards responses to viewer comment. Moreover the only way to test the adequate functioning of a public sphere is to trace it in its effects and to assess the extent to which it assists the participation of citizens in the democratic process. To what extent, for example, does public service broadcasting assist in the development of what Anthony Giddens has called 'dialogic democracy', a mode of resolving disagreement and conflict in both public and private life through discussion and negotiation and not through "pre-established forms of power" (Giddens, 1994: p. 16).

The degree of the BBC's economic independence from national government is not quite matched by its system of internal governance, since the appointment of its governors is subject to the party-political approval of the relevant government minister. In the Thatcher period some critics believed that this political power had been abused in the departure from consensus signalled by the systematic appointment of governors sympathetic to the often controversial views of the Prime Minister. Other countries, for example post-apartheid South Africa, Poland and the Czech Republic, have worked harder to create non-political or at least cross-party 'buffer institutions' between the state and the broadcasters, making such bodies responsible for the approval of appointments to key posts (Republic of South Africa, 1993: p. 16; Jakubowicz, 1996: p. 42).

One other aspect of BBC independence is worth noting. The Peacock Committee was appointed by the Thatcher government to investigate the possible effects of introducing advertising as an alternative method of financing the Corporation. While the Committee's final report advocated a free market approach favouring "a sophisticated market system based on consumer sovereignty" (Peacock, 1986: p. 133), it rejected the option of advertiser finance for the BBC. It was thought that such a change might: "intensify the 'ratings war' and so reduce the effective range of choice open to viewers and listeners" (Peacock, 1986: p. 124). There seems to be some recognition here that the licence fee method of funding has underwritten greater real choice within broadcasting although the concern that advertisers could effectively become censors of content is not voiced.

One of the problems that economists face in considering broadcasting is that it has not functioned, historically, as a true market. With a limited number of channels and prior to the advent of 'pay-per-view' systems, viewers have received whole packages of programmes and so have not made decisions about purchasing particular items. Moreover, there is a continuing problem about the definition of the 'consumer' since commercial broadcasters sell either advertising airtime or audiences to advertisers. In neither case is the audience the consumer and in the second instance the audience becomes neither citizen nor consumer but commodity. The Peacock Report does note some of the difficulties of a free market approach and includes an argument in favour of public subsidy, should the licence fee be abolished, since there would be some "programmes of merit which would not survive in a market where audience ratings was the sole criterion" (Peacock, 1986: p. 148). The Committee also praised some of the features of the existing system in which broadcasters have:

> ... provided packages of programmes to audiences at remarkably low cost... We can also pay tribute to the way in which the packaging of programmes has satisfied and developed audience tastes. The inter-twining of information, education and entertainment has broadened the horizons of great numbers of viewers and listeners. (Peacock, 1986: p. 131)

(ii) The regulation of commercial television

Peacock's compliment to the British broadcasters on the issue of their diversity and cultural quality was intended to refer to commercial or independent television (ITV) as well as to the BBC. But the Report, generally sympathetic to deregulatory philosophies, shows little recognition of the value of the often relatively hidden work of broadcasting regulation. Nor does it fully recognise the role which a regulator can play in furthering the public interest of viewers by standing between broadcaster and advertiser. In Britain this regulatory activity has provided the framework within which programme diversity and some measure of cultural pluralism might be sustained within advertiser-financed broadcasting. I shall concentrate on two aspects of regulation here: firstly, the setting of standards on diversity and quality and secondly, the operation of the code on impartiality.

Since the 1990 Broadcasting Act the Independent Television Commission (ITC) has been the regulator of all commercial, satellite and cable television channels based within the United Kingdom. The Act requires the ITC to ensure the provision of services on ITV which are:

> ... of high quality and offer a wide range of programmes calculated to appeal to a variety of tastes and interests. (Broadcasting Act, 1990: p. 2)

In awarding licences to the ITV companies the ITC was further required to ensure that applicants passed a 'quality threshold' in their programme plans and that they had sufficient financial resources to carry out those plans. It is, arguably, this power to scrutinise business plans that shifts the regulatory process from the realms of the abstract and ideal to those of the concrete and particular. On the content or genre front, the law requires licencees to provide programmes in the categories of news and current affairs, regional pro-grammes, children's programmes and religious programmes. When the ITC issued its own guidelines to applicants it elaborated upon the wording in the Act to require programming in a further six areas: drama, entertainment, sport, factual programmes, education and arts (Independent Television Commission, 1991: p. 29-31). Moreover the regulator made clear what it regarded as the minimum amounts of time to be devoted to programmes in all these categories.

The objective of the Conservative government had been to create a new 'light touch' regulatory framework, but the history of strong regulation and of positive programming obligations within British television culture resulted in a surprising degree of acceptance of the requirements outlined above, and no legal challenge was issued against them. Although, of course, the intensified competition that the new multi-channel age has brought has inevitably changed some of the priorities and patterns of expenditure since the ITV licences were awarded in 1991. It should also be noted that the ITC, unlike its predecessor, has no powers over scheduling, consequently the commercial operators are now able to move what they perceive to be the unpopular programmes to the edges of the schedule and into the margins of lower production budgets. It is the complex interaction of regulatory requirements and the responses of commercial operators to increased market competition that together determine the resourcing of choice, and in turn the wealth or poverty of the public sphere, considered in both material and cultural terms.

On the difficult issue of high quality programmes, how to make them and how to recognise them, the ITC attempted a definition. Such programmes might 'have a special one-off character', they might exhibit 'marked creative originality' or 'exceptionally high production standards'. Those who sought high quality through the production of risky and innovative work which failed should not be penalised for attempting this. The Commission also spoke up for conjoining the popular and the excellent, warning against what the BBC was elsewhere to identify as the lure of the 'Himalayan option' of elite minority programmes; high quality was expected every bit as much to characterise programmes of 'wide audience appeal' (ITC, 1991). Through these sorts of formulations the ITC attempted to provide more detailed guidance on the rather abstract legal reference to 'high quality', monitoring programme output through an annual review of performance and giving thereby some comfort both to discriminating audiences and to ambitious and innovative writers and programme makers.

Programme expenditure, its range and quality, has clear implications for the health of the public sphere. But it is the legal requirement for impartiality in British commercial broadcasting that has most obvious regulatory impact on the political and democratic process. The 1990 Act requires the ITC to ensure that in the case of all licensed services (and this includes satellite and cable channels):

> ... due impartiality is preserved on the part of the person providing the service as respects matters of political or industrial controversy or relating to current public policy. (Broadcasting Act, 1990: p. 6)

The owners of television channels, unlike the owners of newspapers, are thereby prohibited from editorialising on controversial matters, effectively barred from taking advantage of their access to a large soap box to promulgate one set of arguments at the expense of another. At the time of the passing of this law the impartiality clauses caused considerable disquiet among broadcasters who feared that a censoring process might be at work and that these clauses might have what in the United States would be called a 'chilling effect' upon public debate. In 1987, the American Federal Communications Commission had suspended the operation of the 'Fairness Doctrine' in the interests of the free speech rights of television owners. Interestingly the British debate was not about the rights of owners but rather more about the rights of journalists and of audiences to have access to a wide range of often controversial views.

The ITC's guidelines on impartiality have offered some reassurance to programme-makers indicating, for example, that strongly opinionated 'personal view' programmes are still possible, as long as these are balanced by other programmes in a series. The moral questions raised in reporting situations of civil conflict (for example, the war in Bosnia) have recently become an issue in Britain as the war reporter Martin Bell has called for a taking of sides in a perceived larger conflict between good and evil. Interestingly the Act itself acknowledges some limits to impartiality: "...due impartiality does not require absolute neutrality on every issue or detachment from fundamental democratic principles" (Broadcasting Act, 1990: p. 7). This view is confirmed in the ITC Code which stresses that while due impartiality must be applied in reporting controversies on all major matters this:

> ... does not mean that 'balance' is required in any simple mathematical sense or that equal time must be given to each opposing point of view, nor does it require absolute neutrality on every issue. Judgement will always be called for. (ITC, 1995: p. Section 3)

We can only assess the contribution that the code on impartiality makes to the creation of a pluralistic public sphere by considering particular examples of broadcasting practice and by looking at the ways in which programme makers respond to varying corporate, political and economic pressures. This work of testing, monitoring and assessing is beyond the scope of this paper but is starting to be undertaken by some of the associations of civil society which seek a voice in relationship to broadcasting policy and practice (Sargant, 1992; Mitchell and Blumler, 1994).

(iii) Pluralism and minority interests: the example of Channel 4

One last example of legal intervention in the interests of cultural pluralism should be mentioned here. The British Channel 4 is a possibly unique example of a broadcaster financed entirely by advertising, controlled by a Board appointed by the regulatory authority, and with a public remit that excludes the goal of profitability while including the goal of experiment, innovation and the serving of minority interests. It is all the more remarkable that this institution was created by a Conservative government committed to free market principles, and that its virtuous commitment to the often controversial and the sometimes obscure has not prevented it from joining the ranks of the financially successful.

The 1980 Broadcasting Act specified three key objectives for the then new channel. It was to '...encourage innovation and experiment in the form and content of programmes' and to include:

> ... a suitable proportion of matter calculated to appeal to tastes and interests not generally catered for by ITV...[and]

> ... a suitable proportion of programmes...of an educational nature. (Broadcasting Act, 1980)

It is the legal obligation to complement and provide alternatives to what is available elsewhere in the broadcasting system that is perhaps the most innovative aspect of Channel 4's remit and the one that, potentially, makes it an especially valuable contributor to the process of constructing a vigorous public sphere.

In concluding, I make one final point. In the case of any laws, constitutions, professional principles or codes it is the social consequences, the actual political and cultural practice that matters, not what is written on paper. And the final judgement — whether on the value of a broadcasting system or the nature of the good society — must be made not by those with the power to represent others (writers, politicians, programme makers) but by the citizens of the democracy who are also the users of the public sphere. This coming to judgement can only be achieved if there is equal access to a vibrant, pluralistic and adequately resourced public sphere, and if this sphere is moved by the force of argument and ideas and not exclusively by the force of political or corporate power.

Notes

I should like to thank the librarians at Sheffield Hallam University for helping me to locate materials in an unfamiliar area. I am also grateful to the organisers of the 1997 Conference of the British Leisure Studies Association: 'Leisure, Culture and Commerce' where this paper was first delivered.

1 The 1995 figures for terrestrial television are based on a combination of the value of the BBC licence fee (£1.8 billion) together with advertising income for Channel 3 and Channel 4 (£2.1 billion). The third terrestrial channel to be wholly financed by advertising, Channel 5, only began broadcasting in 1997. The Parliamentary grant to the Arts Council in 1995 was £186 million which, re-expressed in billions of pounds, gives us the useful comparative figure of £0.18 billion (Arts Council, 1995: p. 50).

2 Extracts from the ITC documents, Invitation to Apply for Regional Channel 3 Licences and from the Programme Code section on 'impartiality' can be found in J Corner and S Harvey (eds) Television Times, London: Arnold, pp. 234-5; 243-5.

References

Adorno, T. (1991) *The culture industry. Selected essays on mass culture*, edited by J M Bernstein. London: Routledge.

Adorno, T. and Horkheimer, M. (1977) 'The culture industry: Enlightenment as mass deception', in J. Curran *et al.* (eds), *Mass communication and society*. London: Edward Arnold, pp. 349-383.

Advertising Association (1996) *Lifestyle pocket book 1996*. Henley-on-Thames: NTC Publications.

Arts Council of England (1995) *Annual Report 1994/95*. London: Arts Council.

Blumler, J. G. and Nossiter, T. (eds) (1991) *Broadcasting finance in transition*. New York: Oxford University Press.

British Broadcasting Corporation (1992) *Extending choice. The BBC's role in the new broadcasting age*. London: BBC.

———— (1996) *Annual Report and Accounts 1995-96*. London: BBC.

———— (1997) *Annual Report and Accounts 1996-97*. London: BBC.

British Film Institute (1993) *Film and television handbook 1994*. London: BFI.

———— (1994) *Film and television handbook 1995*. London: BFI.

———— (1996) *Film and television handbook 1997*. London: BFI.

Broadcasting Act 1980. London: HMSO.

Broadcasting Act 1990. London: HMSO.

Cohen, J. and Arato, A. (1994) *Civil society and political theory*. Cambridge, Massachusetts: the MIT Press.

Congdon, T. *et al.* (1992) *Paying for broadcasting: The handbook*. London: Routledge.

Corner, J. and Harvey, S. (eds) (1996) *Television times. A reader*. London: Arnold.

———— (1991) *Enterprise and heritage. Cross currents of national culture*. London: Routledge.

Garnham, N. (1990) *Capitalism and communication. Global culture and the economics of information*. London: Sage.

———— (1993) 'The media and the public sphere' in C Calhoun (ed) *Habermas and the public sphere*. Cambridge, Massachusetts: MIT Press, pp 359-376.

Giddens, A. (1994) *Beyond Left and Right. The future of radical politics*. Cambridge: Polity Press.

Greater London Council (1985) *The London industrial strategy*. London: Greater London Council.

Habermas, J. (1979) 'The public sphere' in A Mattelart and S. Siegelaub (eds), *Communication and Class Struggle*, Vol.1, New York: International General.

——— (1989) *The structural transformation of the public sphere*. Cambridge: Polity Press; first published in German in 1962.

——— (1993) 'Further reflections on the public sphere', in C. Calhoun (ed) *Habermas and the public sphere*. Cambridge, Massachussets: MIT Press, pp 421-461.

Harvey, S. (1988) *Cultural Industries, Vols I and II. Interim and Final Reports to Sheffield City Council*. Sheffield: Sheffield City Polytechnic.

Havel, V. (1987) *Living in truth*. London: Faber and Faber.

Hutton, W. (1996) *The state we're in*. London: Vintage.

Independent Television Commission (1991) *Invitation to Apply for Regional Channel 3 Licences*. London: ITC.

——— (1995) *Programme Code*. London: ITC.

——— (1997) *Annual Report and Accounts 1996*. London: ITC.

Jakobowicz, K. (1996) 'Between politicisation and commercialisation: public service broadcasting in Central and Eastern Europe', *Intermedia*, Vol. 24, No. 6, December/January, 1996-97, pp. 41-42.

Keane, J. (1984) *Public life and late capitalism: Toward a socialist theory of democracy*. Cambridge: Cambridge University Press.

——— (1988) (ed) *Civil society and the state. New European perspectives*. London: Verso.

Kelly, G., Kelly, D. and Gamble, A. (1997) (eds) *Stakeholder capitalism*. London: MacMillan.

Leisure Consultants (1997) *Leisure Forecasts 1997-2001. Leisure in the home*. Sudbury, Suffolk: Leisure Consultants.

Lewis, J. (1990) Art, Culture and Enterprise. The Politics of Art and the Cultural Industries. London: Routledge.

Marcuse, H. (1964) *One dimensional Man. Studies in the ideology of advanced industrial society*. Boston: Beacon Press.

Mitchell, J. and Blumler, J. *et al.* (eds) (1994) *Television and the viewer interest. Explorations in the responsiveness of European broadcasters*. London: John Libbey.

Mulgan, G. and Worpole, K. (1986) *Saturday night or Sunday morning? From arts to cultural industry — New forms of cultural policy*. London: Comedia.

Myerscough, J. (1988) *The economic importance of the arts in Britain.* London: Policy Studies Institute.

Peacock Committee (1986) *Report of the Committee on Financing the BBC,* Cmnd. 9824. London: HMSO.

Perkin, H. (1989) *The rise of professional society. England since 1880.* London: Routledge.

Price, M. (1995) *Television, the public sphere and national identity.* Oxford: Clarendon Press.

Republic of South Africa (1993) *Independent Broadcasting Authority Act,* Government Gazette, Vol 340, Cape Town, 27 October.

Sargant, N. (1992) *Broadcasting Policy: Listening to the consumer. The case for a Broadcasting Consumer Council — A discussion paper.* London: Consumers' Association.

Smith, A. (1993) 'What are the arts for?', *From books to bytes. Knowledge and information in the postmodern era.* London: British Film Institute.

Varley, N. (1997) 'Mellor targets Sky squeeze on soccer fans', *Guardian,* 16 August.

Vickerman, R. W. (1983) 'The contribution of economics to the study of leisure', *Leisure Studies,* 2: pp. 345-64.

Williams, R. (1966) *Culture and society 1780-1950.* Harmondsworth: Penguin Books; first published in 1958.

Mega-Events and Modernity

International Expositions and the Construction of Public Culture

Maurice Roche

Sheffield University

Introduction

This paper is concerned with the influence of great cultural events, or 'mega-events', on the construction of public culture in Western modernity, at both the national and the international levels[1]. It concentrates in particular on the paradigmatic genre of the great international cultural event, namely the international exposition. The view taken in this paper is that Expos promoted consumer culture and many features of popular culture which we now associate with "post-modern culture" (e.g. Featherstone, 1992). However they did so during historical periods, namely the late 19thC and early 20thC, normally associated with the development rather than transcendence of 'modernity'. This view, which I explore in greater detail elsewhere[2] and which has some resonances with other analysts' views (e.g. Rojek, 1996), is that, ironically, from the very beginning the modernisation process contained many features associated with 'post'-modernity. So in exploring Expos we are exploring what might be seen as the 'archaeology' of 'post-modern' culture and putting it into perspective as a development within (late) modern culture with many precedents and roots in the modernization process, rather than as some virtually unprecedented radical transformation of modern culture into something other than it.

Expos, 'modern culture' and 'post-modern culture': institutions and attitudes

Late 19thC and early 20thC international expo events provided a new kind of public arena, a new kind of public time and place, for a new type of public to recognise itself in, participate in and use. These public arenas were pre-structured by elite and ideological versions of 'knowledge' and 'education' and of who to include and exclude in the micro-politics of event production. To consider this production dimension, and the ways in which

33

this pre-structuring was or was not contested in the micro-politics of event attendance, is evidently of importance to a general understanding of the social history and sociology of expos. However these issues cannot be addressed here given space limitations (see Roche, 1999). Instead in this paper I will address the fact of the recurrent massive popularity and attractiveness of these expos to the mass publics of many Western nations as forms of leisure. To do this I will focus on their 'entertainment' and 'consumer cultural' aspects rather than on their more (at least nominally) 'educational' and often explicitly ideological and propagandist aspect[3].

It was in the rise of the expo as mass popular entertainment form that many of the institutions that we are familiar with in contemporary popular culture — a culture sometimes characterised as 'post-modern' — arguably had their origins. Contemporary popular culture is effectively a changing mixture of 'modern' and 'post-modern' forms and themes. The former relates to the processes of homogenisation and massification connected with the building of nation-states and nationally and imperially-based industrial capitalist economies as work-based societies, and it is most strongly connected with periods of initial 'modernization'. The latter relates to the processes of individualisation and de-massification connected with the late 20thC reconstruction of the state and capitalism, towards multi-tiered political and regulatory institutions, information and services-based economies, oriented to consumption and animated by global and technological factors and forces. The contemporary combination of, among others, the national, imperial, industrial and 'work-driven' elements comprising 'modern culture' and, among others, the post-national, post-colonial, post-industrial and consumerist/leisure-oriented elements comprising 'post-modern culture', not to mention the dynamics and tensions between these formations, has its origins in a similar combination of formations in late 19thc popular culture, which can be seen most clearly in the great expos of the period.

The 'modern' and 'post-modern' elements and formations of popular culture indicated above, in spite of their tensions and contradictions nonetheless, since their development in the late 19thC, have typically been connected through various sets of cultural institutions and cultural industries. The development of schools, teaching professions, publicly funded schooling systems, national curriculum programmes and the progressive extension of obligatory attendance to older aged children and young people in the late 19thC and early 20thC was evidently connected with nation-building, 'modernization' processes and the construction of 'modern' public culture. Something similar could be said about the initial developments of 'national' or 'public' broadcasting, first radio and then TV, in the 1920 to 1960 period. However, another set of cultural institutions and 'industries', arguably, has had as much societal impact and significance in modernity as national schooling and broadcasting systems.

This institutional set includes museums, art galleries, department stores, theme parks and large scale fairs. Their development as aspects of popular culture was either anticipated, or given crucial boosts, by the late 19thC series of international expos. Compared with the rigidities and relentlessly 'modern cultural' character of much of state-based schooling and broadcasting, Expos provided a flexibility, particularly in their interconnections with the international expo movement, which allowed them to be turned and used by people to engage in public culture in either, or (intermittently) in both, 'modern' and 'post-modern' ways.

We need to consider the main types of public behavioural and attitudinal styles and repertoires which influenced peoples' ways of orienting to and using these cultural forms and institutions in their visits to expos. These attitudes and practices can be characterized as involving popular cultures of 'urban cosmopolitanism', and also more generally 'touristic consumerism'. These two sets of attitudes and values are interconnected and they had as much to do with the international dimension of these events as with their national dimension. They are consistent with, and anticipate, many features of contemporary 'post-modern' culture.

In this paper I will first discuss some important perspectives relevant to understanding the development of late 19thC public culture in general and mega-events, especially expos, focusing in particular on Hobsbawm's account of 'invented traditions'. I will then give an overview of late 19thC and early 20thC expos. Finally I will outline some of the main cultural impacts of expos, focusing on impacts on the development of consumer culture including 'touristic consumerism', particularly in the spheres of urban culture and the growth of 'urban cosmopolitanism' in popular urban culture.

Perspectives on public culture in late 19thC

The construction of national and international public culture in the late 19th century

From mid-19thC to the start of the First World War some of the main institutions of modernity were formed in Western societies. These institutions were developed in nationstate-based societies, societies which were organized by means of a large-scale state and military apparatus, containing and regulating a constantly growing and self-transforming industrial capitalist economy, and legitimated by the slow and contested growth of democratic politics. Nationstate societies located themselves, and recognised, identified and differentiated themselves, in terms of an unregulated and conflict-ridden multi-national world context, involving hierarchies of nations together with their empires and colonies.

Alongside of these institutional developments and dynamics, and interconnected with them, new public spheres and popular forms of national culture developed within nationstates. These were influenced on the one hand by 'official' governmental and other elite ideologists for the new order and by the politico-cultural movements influenced by them, and on the other hand by democratic and other (e.g. socialist, feminist, consumerist etc.) processes and socio-political movements among the mass of the new 'publics'.

These processes have not always been understood and analysed as episodes in the 'social construction of public culture' which is how I prefer to see them. This is because on the one hand they can appear to be over-influenced by power elites and their interests, while on the other they can appear to be non-rational domains of symbol, myth and emotion, not open on either account to rational-discursive and democratic politics. However, while these factors undoubtedly framed and influenced national public spheres, civil societies and their arenas of debate and conflict, they did not exhaust them in principle, and in practice their influence was as often weak and contradictory as it was strong and coherent.

Nevertheless the construction of national public spheres and civil societies in the form of national public cultures is well-trodden ground in social and political theory, having been well researched in studies of the 'imagining' of national communities (Anderson, 1991), the "invention of tradition" (Hobsbawm and Ranger, 1984), the building of national cultures (e.g. Gellner, 1983; Smith, 1971, 1995) and also in more specialist studies of the social history of nations' cultural institutions and industries (of education, the press, leisure, sport and so on). From the point of view of this paper it is worth noting how much of the substance of these sorts of studies of the formation of national culture refer to large scale events which may have a spectacular ritual, dramatic or festive character to them. And indeed, there is substantial research on the nation-building roles of large scale public events[4].

However the inter-national dimension of these nation-building and public culture-building processes, which is also characteristic of modern societies, has not been as well understood or studied (on sport see Houlihan, 1994). Hence one of my interests in this paper is to illuminate the origins and formation of inter-national public culture through examining the nature and role of inter-national mega-events in particular. This inter-national dimension, and thus inter-national public culture, refers to four related phenomena. Firstly it refers to public images of divers subordinate nationalities, ethnicities or religious groups (which may include immigrant/diaspora groups and/or membership in transnational religious communities, hence the inter-nationalism) within any given nation; secondly it refers to national publics' images of and attitudes to 'other nations' ('foreigners', difference etc.); thirdly it refers to images of 'inter-national society' and transnational universalistic principles and practices (such as human rights etc.) held by the members of any given national public as part of their conception of their own civil society and public sphere. Fourthly it refers to the sphere in which national governments' foreign policies, inter-governmental organizations, inter-national non-governmental organizations (INGOs) and multi-national capitalist corporations (MNCs) operate, particularly with respect to culture and communications. What I hope to show in my research on Expos and Olympics[5] is that many aspects of this concept of inter-national public culture have been affected by the development of these mega-events and of the event movements associated with them. To help develop the terms of this discussion, and before we move to the concrete history of Expos, we can now briefly consider a notable and relevant analysis of late 19thC public culture, namely Eric Hobsbawm's (1992) account of 'mass-produced traditions'.

Hobsbawm's influential account of the 'invention of traditions', indeed their 'mass-production' in the late 19thC, from the point of view of the concerns of this paper is effectively an account of the social construction of public culture. One of its many strengths, unlike many nationally-based histories, is that it is comparative, surveying Britain, France, Germany and the USA. Thus, while it does not aim to provide a systematic social theory of these construction processes it is relevant to broad sociological concerns about the nature of Western 'modernity', 'modernization' and social dynamics in this period firstly by drawing on and applying neo-Marxist analysis of the relevance of capitalist dynamics and state-building for class relations, particularly between the new middle classes and the working class, to the sphere of culture, and secondly through the comparative historical information it provides.

Allowing for many national historical differences, particularly in Europe, related to the uneven development of industrialisation and/or nationhood Hobsbawm's account shows the development of similar patterns of popular and public cultural institution-creation by governmental and middle class elites in late 19thC Europe and the USA. These patterns emerged in response to the new political situation created by democratisation, the often fraught process of extending citizenship and voting rights first to men and (much) later to women in the USA and Europe from the 1870s onwards. Western governments and their states in general now need to be legitimised by popular consent. This in turn created powerful interests on the part of national 'establishments', ruling elites and middle classes to attempt to channel and control the development of working class consciousness, demands and behaviour by means other than coercion. There was a need to win the 'hearts and minds' of newly enfranchised working-class 'citizens' for projects of economic growth and nation-building.

This led to a variety of what we would now call 'cultural policies' (McGuigan, 1995), and in particular 'cultural inclusion' policies and initiatives, by political and economic elites to involve the mass of the people in new cultural institutions and cultural industries. The most tangible and institutionalised of these from the 1870s was probably the development of universal compulsory primary, and later secondary, schooling in a nationally determined and characterised curriculum of the skills and knowledge, attitudes and behaviour appropriate for new 'citizens'.

In addition the new citizens could be attracted to participate in, on the one hand, new forms of official/national culture and 'civil religion' — appealing to public interests in collective identity, meaning and purpose — and, on the other hand, to civil society-based forms of popular culture and cultural industries — appealing to workers' growing interests in re-creation, escape from work, entertainment and consumption. Of these cultural policies

Hobsbawm (1992) writes: "To establish the clustering of 'invented traditions' in western countries between 1870 and 1914 is relatively easy" (p. 303). Examples were "old school ties and jubilees, Bastille Day and the Daughters of the American Revolution, May Day, the Internationale and the Olympic Games, ... the Cup Final and Tour de France as popular rites, and the institution of flag worship in the USA" (p. 303).

While Hobsbawm focuses on official and elite-inspired 'popular cultural' policy he also recognises that there was a variable reception of 'invented traditions' by national publics, and thus that some of them failed. Further, new traditions were also created by class-based rather than nation-based popular movements, for instance the revival or invention of 'folk' costume among the peasantry, class-specific festivals such as May Day (created in 1890: pp. 283-8) and migrant sub-cultures among the working class, and exclusive class-specific sports among the middle class (p. 305/6)[6].

The account of the history of national and international public culture and public events which I try to develop in my work (see Roche, 1998) emphasizes the importance of three categories of mass spectacle and their interconnection — namely mass rituals and festivals, mass sport events including the Olympics, and mass participation in Expositions. Hobsbawm's survey touches on each of these three key categories. Firstly he touches on Expositions in the context of a discussion of official cultural policy in France in the 1870-1914 period.

Coming out of the crises of 1870 — a national defeat in the Franco-Prussian war and what was effectively a civil war in the Paris Commune — the new Third Republic embarked on a major series of cultural policies to consolidate itself with the public. Three policies in particular are worth noting. Firstly there was the creation of primary education "a secular equivalent to the church ... imbued with revolutionary and republican principles and content, and conducted by the secular equivalent of the priesthood"...."to turn peasants into Frenchmen and ... Frenchmen into good Republicans" (Hobsbawm, 1992: p. 271). Secondly there was "the mass production of public monuments", particularly of the female figure 'Marianne', symbol of the French Revolution, and local politicians, which virtually amounted to "statue mania" (p. 272) and which became focal points for official ceremonies. Finally there was "the invention of public ceremonies" including official and unofficial festivities connected with special holidays in the national calendar such as Bastille Day, created in 1880. On this and other similar uses of the symbols and heritage of the French Revolution for the purposes of a new wave of nation-building Hobsbawm observes that the general tendency of this kind of policy "was to transform the heritage of the Revolution into a combined expression of state pomp and power and the citizens" pleasure" (p. 271) In this connection, then, it is worth noting that the Third Republic was responsi-ble for three of the biggest and most important of the late 19thC series of International Expositions, namely those staged in Paris in 1878, 1889 and 1900, and we will consider these in a little more detail later in this chapter. In this regard Hobsbawm (1992: p. 271) notes in passing: "A less permanent form of public celebration were the occasional world expositions which gave the Republic the legitimacy of prosperity, technical progress — the Eiffel Tower — and the global colonial conquest they took care to emphasize" (see also Harris, 1975; Mandell, 1967).

Secondly, regarding sport, Hobsbawm notes that among the entertainment-oriented newly 'invented' cultural forms in the 1870-1914 period sport was undoubtedly "the most significant of the new social practices" (p. 298). In the case of Germany mass gymnastic movements, and their events and festivals, had throughout the 19thc been associated with nationalism, and particularly so in the nation-building period following German unification in 1870 (e.g. Guttman, 1994; Hoberman, 1984; Mosse, 1975). However British-originated elite and mass sport forms, movements and events, complemented by American and French developments of both nationally-specific (American football, baseball, mass cycling) and international (Olympic) sports, rapidly became very important in all of the societies surveyed. They provided important cultural institutions for promoting national identity whether through national specificity or through inter-national competition (Hobsbawm, 1992: pp. 300/1), as well as providing the opportunity for the creation of more exclusive and divisive class-specific cultures and identities (on the international dimension of sport see Houlihan, 1994).

Thirdly there is the issue of the development of mass rituals and festivals[7]. Here Hobsbawm notes in relation to late 19thC public culture and invented traditions, that one particular "idiom of public symbolic discourse", — namely 'the theatrical', in the form of "Public ceremonies, parades and ritualized mass gatherings"— had a lasting influence on early and mid-20thC politics and history (see also Mosse, 1975). While recognizing that such events were "far from new" he observes that "their extension for official purposes and for unofficial secular purposes (mass demonstrations, football matches, and the like) in this period is rather striking" (Hobsbawm, 1992: p. 305). They were connected with "the construction of formal ritual spaces", and "this appears to have been systematically undertaken even in countries which had hitherto paid little attention to it". This period saw "the invention ... of substantially new constructions for spectacle and de facto mass ritual such as sports stadia, outdoor and indoor" (p. 305). The use of these constructions "anticipate[d] the development of formal spaces for public mass ritual (the Red Square from 1918) which was to be systematically fostered by fascist regimes" (p. 305) and (as he indicates in the reference to Red Square) by communist regimes, in the inter-war period.

In summary, then, Hobsbawm's analysis is comparative and thematic, so it does help to illuminate the inter-national dimension of public culture in the late 19thC. However it is mainly concerned with national traditions and national class relations. So inevitably the picture of the development of international public culture which it provides is limited.

My line of analysis in this section and in the paper more generally (also in Roche, 1998) is that the development of great public events in the late 19thC, particularly the International Expos, and arising out of them the

Olympic Games, together with the event movements and networks and cycles
connected with them decisively influenced and help create a new level and
form of inter-national public culture. However Expos themselves need to be
understood as contextualised in a broader set of cultural and political cultural
movements and developments in national cultural policy in the late 19thC.
This has already been indicated in my discussion of Hobsbawm. In terms of
political culture, the background of all other movements in the late 19thC
consisted of movements connected with the various versions of nationalism
and nation-state-building in Europe, North America and South America in
particular (and with the various versions of imperialism connected with them)
are an important background and resource for the cultural movements we
are mainly concerned with.

Evidently nationalism was closely intertwined with the developing power
structures of states and governments and greatly influenced the sphere of
culture. But we should also bear in mind that other socio-political movements, without comparable direct access to state power, were also important
elements and actors in the political environment, both nationally and
internationally, in particular trade unionism and socialism, and these also
had some presence and influence in the arenas of public culture and in the
history and construction of public culture[8].

The late 19thC cultural movements under discussion here were in large
part 'rational recreation' movements concerned in large part, although not
exclusively, with sport (including physical education and training, mass
gymnastics and Olympics within this as well as British-originated sports and
other national sports). To a lesser extent 'rational recreation' was also
connected with the development of tourism as a form of education as well
as entertainment. These cultural movements were also connected with
religious and religiously-related movements, such as 'muscular Christianity'
in the sphere of sport and 'temperance' in the spheres of sport and tourism.
We must now turn to give a picture of the main form of mega-event we are
concerned with in this paper, namely the late 19thC and early 20thC Expos.

International expositions and public culture 1851-1939

Overview

International expos were a very significant cultural institution both for the
host city and nation, and also for the international community, throughout
the period 1851 to 1939[9]. They were held every few years, barring periods
of major war, in one nation or another in Europe or in the USA throughout
this period. Allowing for ambiguities in the definition of an international
expo, roughly 15-20 major events were staged in the 1850-1914 period, and
5-10 were staged in the 1918-1939 inter-war period. In addition numerous
more specialised or smaller scale international and national events of a
similar general type occurred in nations around the world. There was no
particular planned temporal cycle or circulation of sites for the major events,

but, because of their scale and costs, they were rarely staged more frequently than 5 to 10 years in each of the major countries, namely Britain, France and the USA. We can now briefly review these three major countries.

The British, who created the genre in the 1851 'Crystal Palace' inter-national exhibition, had planned to hold one every decade, but after their 1862 expo, their approach to these events changed and the French, and later the Americans, effectively took over the leadership of the expo genre. In the 1870s the British staged Specialist Exhibitions virtually every year. From the 1880s to the first World War, besides the two Victoria Jubilee festivals (1887 and 1897), the British held a number of Imperial expos and festivals and expos (e.g. 1886, 1899, 1908-1914 period), and re-animated this imperial version of the inter-national expo genre in the inter-war year with big events at Wembley 1924/5 and Glasgow 1938. The French, in particular the city of Paris, took the leadership of the genre over from the 1850s through to 1900 with five major events in Paris, one in each decade (1855, 1867, 1878, 1889, 1900). Interestingly the French and Parisian elites appear to have been exhausted and jaded by their 1900 Expo (Mandell, 1967). Aside from various smaller scale events, they did not stage another expo for a generation, until the series in the inter-war period (i.e. Marseilles 1922; Paris 1925, 1931, 1937). The Americans were preoccupied with the Civil War in the 1860s and with reconstruction thereafter. Setting aside their small-scale copy of the 1851 event in New York in 1852, understandably they did little in terms of major exhibitions in the 1850s and 60s. However they then produced a series of five major events from the 1870s to the First World War (Philadelphia 1876, Chicago 1893; St. Louis 1904; San Francisco 1915) and four in the inter-war period (Philadelphia 1926; Chicago 1933; San Francisco 1939 and New York 1939/40) together with a mass of USA regional and state-based national-level events throughout these periods.

National governments were always significantly involved in the organization of these events. They were also always involved, to a greater or lesser extent, in the financing of these events, which often made considerable losses. In spite of that fact, and whatever the state of the economic cycle, whether boom or slump, national governments continued to encourage and sponsor these official forms of grand public spectacle and theatre. National governments understood that expos, if successful, offered a platform for the inter-national projection of positive images of their nation. Success could be better assured if nations copied successful models and attempted to improve on them in terms of the quantity or quality of previously successful elements. This inter-country and inter-city competitiveness and 'leap-frogging' was clear in the relations between the London and Paris expos of the 1850s and 60s, and again in the relation between the Paris and American expos of 1889 to 1904.

The cultural significance and social role of late 19thC Expos

The Expos were a new and powerful cultural medium for conveying information and values to a mass public. Marshall McLuhan's legendary observation about television, that to a significant extent "the medium is the message" could also be said about Expos. A large part of the excitement, attraction and spectacle of expos derived from the medium itself, namely the main buildings and site architecture together with the huge gatherings of people on an historically unprecedented scale. This was as important as the contents of the exhibition.

However the contents were also spectacular, consisting of huge collections and exhibitions of among other things raw materials from around the world, new productive and communication technologies, new products and commodities, art objects and scientific information. They represented attempts to achieve both an encyclopaedic stock-taking of the current state of knowledge and practice among the advanced industrial societies and also and attempt to communicate and popularise this among mass publics, mainly in the host nation but also through the press and later radio and film, in many nations.

Assessing the Expo genre

An Expo supporter, American President McKinley (who ironically was later shot at Buffalo Expo 1901) optimistically and idealistically summed up the significance of Expositions as follows: "Expositions are the timekeepers of progress. They record the world's advancement. They stimulate the energy, enterprise, and intellect of the people and quicken human genius. They go into the home. They broaden and brighten the daily life of the people. They open mighty storehouses of information to the student. Every exposition, great or small, has helped this onward step" (quoted Rydell, 1984: p. 4). This view summed up the views of many of the political and cultural elites which, in flexible and changing configurations, decided on and created the great series of expo events outlined above. It also sums up the views of many liberal social historians who have written on expos[10].

As against this many other social historians and social observers have been more critical. For instance the Frankfurt School critical theorist Walter Benjamin, writing in 1935 and unfortunately without reference to the great expos of his own day, (e.g. the 1933/4 Chicago expo and plans for the 1937 Paris expo) observed about the late 19thC Paris series that: "World exhibitions were places of pilgrimage to the fetish Commodity." (p. 165) and "Fashion prescribed the ritual by which the fetish Commodity wished to be worshipped" (p. 166). "The workers were to the fore as customers. The framework of the entertainment industry had not yet been formed. The public festival provided it." Generally, the expos "opened up a phantasmagoria into which people entered in order to be distracted. The entertainment industry made that easier for them by lifting them to the level of the commodity. They yielded to its manipulations while enjoying their alienation from themselves and from others" (p. 165).

Two contemporary Exposition historians who acknowledge the real popularity, attraction and memorability of expos for ordinary people throughout the late 19thC and early 20thC (Greenhalgh, 1988: p. 225; Rydell, 1993:

pp. 2-3) nonetheless are equally as critical in their general assessments as Benjamin. Paul Greenhalgh (1988: p. 22) observes: "the genre became a self-perpetuating phenomenon, the extra-ordinary culture spawn of industry and empire". Their purpose was "to indicate civilization was advancing in some known direction" (p. 23) in spite of the often chaotic social changes going on in the relevant periods, "and things would get better. [...] As cultural manifestations, they revealed an expansive West in its most flamboyant and bombastic state; baroque, overblown expressions of societies that felt they ruled the material world absolutely" (p. 24).

Elites used Expos to propagandise nationalism. As Greenhalgh observes: "This penetrated popular cultural forms in all sorts of ways, many of which Expo organisers also used. The exhibitions had to do more than simply whip up general verbal enthusiasm, (MR for nationalism and imperialism), they also had to give physical form to pavilions and palaces and to penetrate higher levels of cultural production with propagandist dogma. They had to cater for the educated as well as the ignorant, providing a formula and a rationale for national culture which was capable of being interpreted by a wide cross-section of the population" (p. 113).

In related vein, Robert Rydell, focusing particularly on the American series of World's Fairs, observes that: "Between 1876 and 1916 a network of international expositions spanned the nation, putting the world on display and shaping the world view of millions of Americans. Without exception, these expositions were upper-class creations initiated and controlled by locally or nationally prominent elites" (Rydell, 1993: p. 235). "To alleviate the intense and widespread anxiety that pervaded the United States [in this period] the directors of the expositions offered millions of fairgoers an opportunity to reaffirm their collective national identity in an updated synthesis of progress and white supremacy that suffused the blueprints of future perfection offered by the fairs" (p. 4). "The influence of America's international expositions permeated the nation's arts, political system, and economic structure. Far from simply reflecting American culture, the expositions were intended to shape that culture. They left an enduring vision of empire" (p. 237).

More generally, Rydell also observes that "the Victorian era fairs played. an important role in shaping the contours of the modern world" (p. 15). They "were part of what became, after the success of London's Crystal Palace Exhibition on 1851, a worldwide movement" (Rydell, 1993: p. 8; also Gilbert in Rydell and Gwinn, 1994).

Expos and cities: Cultural impacts on place and space

In terms of the general themes of this paper the view taken here is that it is a profound mistake about the nature of popular culture in modernity, to imagine that 'consumer culture' and the 'post modern culture' it is associated with somehow emerged 'ex nihilo' in the dying decades of the 20thC. This ignores a century of growth of consumer institutions (department stores, advertising as we will discuss later in this section) which had been introduced in the late 19thC expos and which were continually developed and diffused in the early and mid 20thC — before television took over this role in the post-war period — by the expo movement. Many writers have pointed to the late 19thC expo-based precedents for consumer culture in their studies of late 20thC consumer culture[11].

An important aspect of the cultural significance and impact of the Expo genre in social history of modernity, then, can be summed up the argument that Expos introduced and promoted what can be called a 'touristic consumer culture', a form of popular culture we are familiar with in late 20thC moder-nity (McCannell, 1989; Urry, 1990). As a complex of attitudes comprising a 'popular internationalist' dimension of 'public culture' this involves four main elements, namely: (i) a generalised consumerist orientation to the 'world of commodities'; (ii) an orientation to 'foreign'/'exotic' (internationally sourced) commodities; (iii) an interest in 'foreigners'/'exotic others'; and (iv) an interest in travel and 'excursioning'. An important aspect of this touristic consumer-ism was the development of the fact of, and public interest in, versions of cultural cosmopolitanism in the capital cities and other major cities of the advanced industrial societies of the West from the late 19thC onwards.

Expos, tourist sites and theme parks

Expos played an important role, as tourist attractions, in stimulating domes-tic and international tourism and tourism as a cultural industry from the mid 19thC, and also in stimulating the allied popular cultural world-views of 'touristic consumerism' and 'urban cosmopolitanism'. Expos left their imprint on the late 20thC tourist industry in particular and its touristically permeated popular culture in general not only through their continuing mega-event calendars and 'event heritages' in cities but also through their influence on and connection with an archetypal late 20thC form of tourist attraction, namely the 'theme park'. Expos were (and are) effectively tempo-rary theme parks. The development of theme parks, particularly by the Disney organisation from the late 1950s, and later by many imitators across the world, were, in certain respects, 'permanent expos' and thus could be thought of as 'permanent mega-events'.

Disney theme parks' designed and controlled environments reflected Walt Disney's alleged dislike of the traditional amusement park and New York's Luna Park (Coney Island) in particular (see Kasson, 1978) and on the other hand, he was positively impressed with expos such as those of Chicago 1933 and New York 1939. The contemporary genre of theme parks to which he helped to give birth contain many expo features, and many commentators have noted the influence of the great international expo tradition on the concept of the postwar theme park. For instance Davis (1996) observes: "The roots of the theme park run deep in the history of popular and commercial culture. Its ancestors include the older amusement park and its peripatetic ancestors, the circus and the carnival, but also the industrial expositions and World Fairs of the 19th and 20th centuries" (p. 400). Smoodin, in his collection of studies of Disney, notes: "Disneyland, that homage to the possibilities of the future, really functioned as a further development of the last century's gigantic public spectacles — the Chicago ... Exposition of 1893, for instance" (1994: p.12). This connection is generally visualisable in relation to Disney theme parks. This is particularly so in relation to the EPCOT Centre zone at Disney World in Orlando, Florida, which was opened in 1975, and which is effectively a permanent copy of an international expo.

Expos' impacts on cities

Expos as temporary mega-events and theme parks as permanent mega-events have had, and continue to have, a range of impacts on cities both from the short and long term perspectives. Expos have a more direct and obvious effect on cities since they are traditionally staged either in a prestigious central area of a city, as in the case of the great Paris 19thC expos or, alternatively, in an urban area which the city leadership has zoned for economic development, as in the case of most of the postwar expos, and as is currently the case for the 1998 Lisbon and 2000 London expos for instance.

Expos, seen as temporary model cities and as 'event theme parks', can be analysed as essentially 'ephemeral' phenomena (e.g. Greenhalgh, 1988), leaving little trace on the cities which host them and having little impact beyond the short term. The analogy here might be with the travelling fair or circus, a short-term local and visitor entertainment attraction. In more contemporary experience 'The Big Top' temporary circus arena has its current analogy in international rock stars such as the Rolling Stones and Michael Jackson 'on the road' on 'the world tour' with their huge mobile theatrical stage sets and light shows (Garofolo, 1992).

However this analogy would be misplaced and is misleading. While many expos have indeed left little architectural trace, a number of the 19thc and early 20thC expos left important and distinctive architectural and facilities heritages in their host cities, particularly expos held in the cities of London, Paris and Barcelona. Paris was the most notable of these with many landmark buildings and monuments in central Paris being attributable to the series of expos held there, including the Grand and Petit Palaces, the Palace of Chaillot, a number of bridges over the Seine and, most notably the Eiffel tower which was constructed for the 1889 expo. It is also worth noting that Eiffel contributed to another legendary permanent landmark monument connected with an expo, namely the Statue of Liberty — now so identified with the city of New York and another major tourist attraction. The statue was originally intended to be presented to America on the occasion of the 1876 Philadelphia expo commemorating the American revolution. But this proved impractical for various political, technical and financial reasons. However part of it, namely the torch, was in fact displayed at this expo to help raise public awareness of the project and also funds for it (Bond, 1996; also Harriss, 1975 and Allwood, 1978).

As with earlier expos most post-war expos have usually been expected to feature some unusual monumental architecture and related spectacular 'centrepiece' structures which may or may not be permanent and thus contribute an event heritage. The 'Atomium' structure created for the Brussels 1958 expo, a two hundred feet high lattice of large spheres containing displays, viewing areas and a restaurant, is such a physical event heritage. So too is the 'Space Needle', a tall viewing tower created for the Seattle 1962 expo. Relatedly there is currently a debate in Britain in relation to the Millennium 2000 expo, about the desirability of some permanent event heritage and about the fact that the expo's spectacular, monumental and expensive centrepiece 'Dome' structure has been designed as an essentially temporary facility. On the other hand the London Millennium expo mega-event project incorporates other forms of less visible and non-spectacular permanent physical event heritage which have become an increasingly important aspect of post-war mega-events. These include transportation and infrastructure developments and the reclamation of industrially polluted and/or derelict inner city land for urban regeneration uses, in this case an important but neglected riverside tract of land in the historic and central London area of Greenwich.

These kinds of often non-spectacular physical event heritages through transport and infrastructure development and generally through urban reclamation and regeneration have been evident and important aspects of many post-war expo plans and experiences. For instance the Montreal 1967 expo involved the development of an island area in the St. Lawrence river together with the architecturally innovative 'Habitat' high density housing complex. Comparably, and more currently, the Lisbon 1998 expo involves the regeneration of a declining and derelict riverfront area on the river Tagus next to the new and nationally very important 15 kilometre Vasco da Gama bridge which crosses the river and provides a vital new link between central and southern Portugal[12].

'Urban cosmopolitanism'

This public attitude set is connected with some of the urban place and space issues outlined so far and is also connected with a more general development of 'touristic consumerist' attitude. The quasi-touristic encounter with 'foreigners' at expos contributed to a popular taste for participation in a cosmopolitan dimension of the culture of the times, in addition to participation in a developing but exclusively national form of public culture. Indeed the relevance of cosmopolitanism to his times was a theme the sociologist Durkheim lectured on it at a conference held during the 1900 Paris expo (reported in Lukes, 1975: p. 350).

The cosmopolitanism of the international expo event site was an exaggerated microcosm of the kind of cosmopolitanism characteristic of 19thC an 20thC urbanism, particularly the cultural mixtures present in most capital cities, but also in other large cities, especially those acting as trading and migrant centres. The point that needs to be stressed here, as we have seen above, is that the expos themselves were designed and experienced as 'cities-in-miniature' and as 'ideal cities' etc. Hence the name for Chicago's 1893 site 'the White City' which was also used as the name for one of London's main expo sites in the 1908-14 period.

Public attitudes and practices towards culture were influenced by the growth of a range of new and specifically citycentre-based places and spaces and cultural institutions including museums, art galleries, department stores[13]. Middle class and increasingly mass working class access to and interaction with these institutions in major cities helped to form national publics. Obviously museums, art galleries and fairs antedate 19thC expos and have a long institutional history in Western Europe in particular. However even these were qualitatively transformed by the international expo movement. This resulted, in the case of museums and art galleries, in a new level of popular recognition of and access to institutions which previously were effectively closed and elite-oriented, and in the case of fairs in an increase their scale, the technological complexity of their infrastructure, and their capacity to create, control and sell 'excitement' and extreme emotional stimuli and experiences (cf. de Cauter, 1993). In the other cases, notably department stores and theme parks, these quintessential consumerist and touristic forms and institutions, were either effectively created as concepts by the international expo movement, or their development was rapidly accelerated and widely diffused by them. This set of institutions and industries provided the substantial settings and experiences within expos with which the public — understanding itself in terms of the entertainment frameworks of touristic consumerism and urban cosmopolitanism — interacted, and which repeatedly attracted them to the events in huge numbers.

Conclusion

I will conclude this brief account of 'work-in-progress' on expositions and their cultural significance in the development of modernity with an appropriately brief and summative conclusion. (For further analysis see Roche, 1999.) In this paper I have attempted to highlight their historic importance in the late 19thC and early 20thC. I have also indicated the continuing relevance of the genre in the practice of late 20thC international public culture. Finally I have indicated the importance of understanding this genre of mega-events for the theory of so-called 'post'-modern culture and its often ignored precedents and origins in 19thC and 20thC modernization processes and dynamics.

Notes

1   The notion of 'mega-event' refers to a general category of 'extra-ordinary' large-scale popular cultural events of national and international significance and it includes a number of genres within it such as Expos and Olympics, but also large scale festivals of various kinds. For the purposes of this paper I assume the intuitive comprehensibility of both the category itself and the fact that Expos exemplify the category. For definitions and

typologies of 'mega-events' and, relatedly, 'hallmark events', see Ritchie, 1984; AIEST, 1987, Syme *et al.*, 1989; Hall, 1989, 1992; Getz, 1991; Law, 1993 ch. 6, and Murphy, 1994, as well as my own publications indicated above. My research interests in mega-events originally arose out of consultancy and research work I undertook in the late 1980s connected with the staging of the Olympic-type World Student Games 1991 event in my home city of Sheffield (see Roche, 1992a, 1992b, 1994). So this paper derives from 'work in (slow) progress'. Also for the purposes of this paper I assume the intuitive comprehensibility of the concept of 'public culture' and notions connected with this such as 'the public sphere' and 'citizenship'. For relevant analyses and applications of these notions see Horne, 1986; Chaney, 1993; and McGuigan, 1995, as well as Roche 1992b, 1992c, 1994.

2   The broader analysis of these and other issues is contained in my forthcoming *Mega-Events and Modernity: Expos and Olympics in the Construction of Public Culture*, to be published in 1999. Readers are referred to this for more elaborate discussion of the points, themes and issues in this paper.

3   On the propagandist aspects, see Rydell, 1984, 1993; also McKenzie, 1984 and Greenhalgh, 1988.

4   See References for studies by Lavenda, Rydell, Greenhalgh, Mosse, Brownell, Lane and Spillman.

5   It should be noted here in passing that Expos were of great importance for the creation and development of the Olympics (e.g. MacAloon, 1981) which have grown to play such an important role in late 20thC global public culture in general and global media culture in particular (e.g. Whannel, 1992; Spa *et al.*, 1995). I do not consider this connection further in this paper (but see Roche, 1999 and note 1 above).

6   On 'manipulation of the public' by class-based imperialist propaganda in this period see, e.g., McKenzie, 1984.

7   Discussed at greater length in relation to the super-nationalism of inter-war imperial and totalitarian public events in Roche, 1999.

8   The relevance of the super-national ideologies and cultural policies of imperialism, communism and fascism for the development of public culture and public events in modernity is discussed further in Roche, 1999.

9   For histories see bibliography for studies by Allwood, Benedict, Greenhalgh Luckhurst, Rydell, Schroeder-Gudehus and Rasmussen, Spillman. For studies of particular expos see Bennett, Dimanche, Findling, Harvey, Hinsley, Mandell, McArthur, Pred, Rydell and Gwinn.

10   E.g., Luckhurst, Allwood, Findling.

11 E.g., see Bibliography for studies by Featherstone, Richards, Pred, de Cauter, Zukin, Williams and Richards.

12 Also see studies of the 1986 Vancouver expo, e.g. Ley and Olds, 1988; and of the 1992 Seville expo, e.g. Harvey, 1996.

13 See Bibliography for studies by Hinsley, Lewis, Williams, Richards.

References and bibliography

AIEST (1987) *The role and impact of mega-events and attractions on regional and national tourism development*, AIEST (Association Internationale d'Experts Scientifique du Tourisme). St. Gall, Switzerland.

Allwood, J. (1978) *The great exhibitions*. London: Cassell and Collier.

Anderson, B. (1991) *Imagined communities*. London: Verso.

Benedict, B. (1994) 'Rituals of representation: Ethnic stereotypes and colonized peoples at World's Fairs', ch. 2 in Rydell, R. and Gwinn, N. (eds) *Fair representations: World's Fairs and the modern world*. Amsterdam: VU University Press.

Benedict, B. *et al.* (1983) *The anthropology of World's Fairs*. London: Scolar Press.

Benjamin, W. (1973) 'Grandeville or the World Exhibitions', (original 1935) section III in 'Paris — the Capital of the 19thC', section of his *Charles Baudelaire: A lyric poet in the high era of capitalism*. London: NLB.

Bennett, T. (1988) 'The exhibitionary complex', *New Formations* Vol. 4 (Spring): pp. 73-102.

Bond, L. (1996) *The Statue of Liberty*. Santa Barbara, CA: Albion Publishing Group.

Brownell, S. (1995) *Training the body for China*. Chicago: University of Chicago Press.

Buzard, J. (1993) *The beaten track: European tourism and literature 1800-1918*. Oxford: Clarendon Press.

de Cauter, L. (1993) 'The panoramic ecstacy: On World Exhibitions and the disintegration of experience', *Theory, Culture and Society*, Vol. 10: pp. 1-23.

Chaney, D. (1993) *Fictions of collective life*. London: Routledge.

Davis, S. (1996) 'The theme park: Global industry and cultural form', *Media, Culture and Society*, Vol 18: pp. 399-422.

Debord, G. (1973) *The society of the spectacle*. Detroit: Black and Red.

Dimanche, F. (1994) 'Ten years after: The Louisiana World's Fair legacy in New Orleans', in Murphy, P. (ed) (1994) *Mega-event legacies*. Victoria: Province of British Columbia. pp. 67-87.

Featherstone, M. (1991) *Consumer culture and postmodernism.* London: Sage.

Findling, J. (1994) *Chicago's great world's fairs.* Manchester: Manchester University Press.

Garofolo, R. (ed) (1992) *Rockin' the boat: Mass music and mass movements.* Boston, MA: South End Press.

Gellner, E. (1983) *Nations and nationalism.* Oxford: Blackwell.

Getz, D. (1991) *Festivals, special events and tourism.* New York: Reinhold Van Vostrand.

Greenhalgh, P. (1988) *Ephemeral vistas: The Expositions Universelles; Great Exhibitions and World's Fairs, 1851-1939.* Manchester: Manchester University Press.

Guttman, A. (1994) *Games and empires: Modern sports and cultural imperialism.* New York: Columbia University Press.

Hall, C. M. (1989) 'The politics of hallmark events', in Syme, G., Shaw, B., Fenton. M and Mueller, W. (eds) *The planning and evaluation of Hallmark Events.* Aldershot: Avebury, pp. 3-19.

―――― (1992) *Hallmark tourist events.* London: Bellhaven.

Harriss, J. (1975) *The tallest tower: Eiffel and the Belle Epoque.* Boston: Houghton Mifflin Co.

Harvey, D. (1989) *The condition of postmodernity.* Oxford: Blackwell.

Harvey, P. (1996) *Hybrids of modernity: Anthropology, the nation state and the universal exhibition.* London: Routledge.

Hinsley, C. (1991) 'The world as marketplace: Commodification of the exotic at the World's Columbian Exhibition, Chicago, 1893', ch. 18 in I. Karp and S. Lavine (eds) *Exhibiting cultures: The poetics and politics of museum display.* Washington: Smithsonian Institution Press.

Horne, D. (1986) *The public culture.* London: Pluto Press.

Hoberman, J. (1984) *Sport and political ideology.* London: Heinemann.

Hobsbawm, E. (1992) 'Mass-producing traditions: Europe, 1870-1914', in Hobsbawm and Ranger *op cit.,* pp. 263-308.

Hobsbawm, E. and Ranger, T. (eds) (1992) *The invention of tradition,* (original 1983). Cambridge: Canto, Cambridge University Press.

Houlihan, B. (1994) *Sport and international politics.* Brighton: Harvester/Wheatsheaf.

Kasson, J. (1978) *Amusing the million: Coney Island at the turn of the century.* New York: Hill and Wang.

Lane, C (1981)*The rites of rulers: Ritual in industrial society — the Soviet case.* Cambridge: Cambridge University Press.

Lavenda, R. (1980) 'The Festival of Progress: The globalising world-system and the transformation of the Caracas carnival 1873', *Journal of Popular Culture*, No. 14: pp. 465-475.

Law, C. (1993) *Urban tourism*. London: Mansell.

Lewis, R. (1983) 'Everything under one roof: World's Fairs and department stores in Paris and Chicago', *Chicago History*, Vol. 12, No. 3: pp. 28-47.

Ley, D. and Olds, K. (1988) 'Landscape as spectacle: World's Fairs and the culture of heroic consumption', *Environment and Planning D: Space and Society* 6, 191-212 .

Luckhurst, K. (1951) *The story of exhibitions*. London: The Studio Publications.

Lukes, S. (1975) *Emile Durkheim*. Peregrine, London.

MacAloon, J. (1981) *This great symbol: Pierre de Coubertin and the origins of the Modern Olympic Games*. Chicago: The University of Chicago Press.

——— (1984) 'Olympic Games and the theory of spectacle in modern societies', in J. MacAloon (ed) *Rite, drama, festival, spectacle*. Philadelphia: The Institute of Human Issues.

MacCannell, D. (1989) *The tourist*. London: Macmillan.

MacArthur, C. (1986) 'The Glasgow Empire Exhibition of 1938: The dialectics of national identity', in Bennett, T. (ed) *Popular culture and social relations*. Milton Keynes: Open University Press: pp. 117-134.

MacKenzie, J. (1984) *Propaganda and empire: The manipulation of British public opinion 1880-1960*. Manchester : Manchester University Press, (ch. 4).

Mandell, R. (1967) *Paris 1900: The Great World's Fair*. Toronto: University of Toronto Press.

McGuigan, (1995) *Culture and the public sphere*. London: Routledge.

Mosse, G. (1975) *The nationalization of the masses: Political symbolism and mass movements in Germany*. New York: Howard Fertig.

Murphy, P. (ed) (1994) *Mega-event legacies*. Victoria: Province of British Columbia.

Pred, A. (1990) *Making histories and constructing geographies*. Oxford : Westview Press, (ch. 5 re Stockholm 1900, the background to Expo).

——— (1991) 'Spectacular articulations of modernity: The Stockholm Exhibition of 1897', *Geografiska Annaler* 73 B 1: pp. 45-84.

Richards, T. (1990) *The commodity culture of Victorian England: Advertising and spectacle 1851-1914*. Stanford: Stanford University Press.

Ritchie, B. (1984) 'Assessing the impacts of hallmark events', *Journal of Travel Research*, Vol. 23, No. 2: pp. 2-11.

Roche, M. (1992a) 'Mega-Events and Micro-Modernization', *British Journal of Sociology* Vol. 43: pp. 563-600.

———— (1992b) 'Mega-events and citizenship', *Vrijtijd en Samenleving (Leisure and Society)* Vol. 10, No. 4: pp. 47-67.

———— (1992c) *Rethinking citizenship: Ideology, welfare and change in modern society.* Cambridge: Polity Press.

———— (1994) 'Mega-events and urban policy', *Annals of Tourism Research*, Vol. 21, No. 1: pp. 1-19.

———— (1999) (forthcoming) *Mega-events and modernity: Olympics, world's fairs and the construction of public culture.* London: Routledge.

Rojek, C. (1995) *Decentring leisure.* London: Sage.

Rydell, R. (1984) *All the world's a fair: Visions of empire at American international expositions 1876-1916.* Chicago: University of Chicago Press.

———— (1993) *World of fairs: The Century-of-Progress Expositions.* Chicago: Chicago University Press.

Rydell, R. and Gwinn, N. (eds) (1994) *Fair representations: World's fairs and the modern world.* Amsterdam: VU University Press.

Schroeder-Gudehus, B. and Rasmussen, A. (1992) *Les Fastes du Progres: Les Guides des Exposition Universelles 1851-(1992).* Paris : L'Atelier d'Edition Europeen, Flammarion.

Smith, A. (1971) *Theories of nationalism.* London: Duckworth.

———— (1995) *Nations and nationalism in a global era.* Cambridge: Polity.

Smoodin, E. (1994) *Disney discourse.* London: Routledge.

Spa, M. de M., Rivenburgh, N., and Larson, J. (1995) *Television in the Olympics.* Luton: John Libbey Media.

Spillman, L. (1997) *Nation and commemoration: Creating national identities in the United States and Australia.* Cambridge: Cambridge University Press.

Syme, G., Shaw. B., Fenton, M. and Mueller, W. (eds) (1989) *The planning and evaluation of hallmark events.* Aldershot: Avebury.

Whannel, G. (1992) *Fields in vision: television sport and cultural transformation.* London: Routledge.

Williams, R. 1982 *Dream worlds: Mass consumption in late 19thC France.* Berkeley: University of California Press.

Urry, J. (1990) *The tourist gaze.* London: Sage.

Zukin, S. (1991) *Landscapes of power: From Detroit to Disney World.* Berkeley: University of California Press.

II

Planning Public Sport and Leisure

Progress towards Shaping a Safety Culture in the Leisure Sector

John Hunter-Jones

University of Manchester

A concern for safety is rarely, if at all, identified as one of the main factors which distinguishes the cultural values of a society. It probably appears rather dull, perhaps even negative in its image and unlikely to determine the historical reputation of a people. Who can say whether the Romans or Moguls were safety conscious societies? It may well be, however, that a safety culture is a necessary foundation for a civilised society and that a culture without concern and the willingness to act for the safety of its people is flawed. This paper considers safety as it relates to the majority of non domestic leisure venues, and does not include leisure transport. Much of the work is applicable to Scotland and Northern Ireland, but because of their separate legal systems the article focuses on the English and Welsh experience. The paper focuses on the reality of safety protection afforded to consumers and how this contrasts with their expectations.

Twenty five years ago the Robens Committee on Safety and Health at Work reported after two years of extensive deliberations (Robens, 1972). The report then led to major legislation, The Health and Safety at Work Act 1974 (HSWA 1974) which, it was hoped, would help to secure safety for all persons at places of work, including the public. Workplaces include all premises where employees have access in the course of their work. This Act, more than any other, can be regarded as setting the general safety standards for the leisure sector and providing safety for consumers. Robens philosophy was that the safety of employees and the public was best achieved by the prevention of injury, borne out of workplace concern. Safe systems of work should be in place by imposing general duties (goals) on employers and employees and by providing relevant guidance and regulations. However, all of the duties are qualified by the term "reasonably practicable", which can consider such factors as money, time or trouble [see *Edwards v National Coal Board* (1949); *All England Law Reports* (AllER) 743] and are, consequently, open to interpretation. As a last resort criminal sanctions can be applied where a reckless disregard for safety occurs, this would normally follow the issue of an improvement/prohibition notice (Barrett and Howells, 1993). In reality the authorities normally intervene after a problem has occurred. The right to inspect premises is subject to conditions [HSWA 1974, s. 20] and typically are pre arranged with the management of the organisation. Prosecutions result only in the minority of breaches considered by the Health and Safety Executive (HSE) and Local Authorities. Many bodies provision of leisure activities (e.g. public music and dancing) also need to have a licence or certificate and this is the alternative, and less trusting, system to ensuring safe practice. The article considers these two different approaches in developing a safety culture.

The statistics available on fatalities and injuries from leisure activities are revealing, but must be treated with caution. The HSE produce extensive research on this area, however their information only relates to activities at a workplace. So, for instance, they record that in 1993/94 8 members of the public drowned in swimming pools (HSE, 1994), yet Sports Council figures show that this was only 3% of all drownings in that period (East Midlands Council for Sport and Recreation, 1995). The Office for National Statistics (ONS) records an average of 75 deaths per annum at recreation and sport venues (excluding transport) between 1992-95 (ONS, 1997), yet the average number of deaths recorded by HSE over this period is only 7 per annum across all consumer/leisure activities (HSE, 1997: p. 1). The above two sets of information also indicate that the majority of leisure injuries occur outside a workplace and many accidents take place at venues within the control of voluntary organisations (not covered by HSE, where no employment takes place). However, the statistics produced by the HSE are the best source of information that we have about safe practice in the leisure sector (e.g., see **Table 1**). The HSE do point out, though, that "only 28% of non fatal injuries to employees in the consumer/leisure industry are reported" (HSE, 1997: p. 9). One would expect the figure for the public to be even lower. The HSE statistics use a broad category of Consumer/Leisure Services (C/L), but within that have specified Sporting and Recreational Activities (SRA). As one might expect 94% of major injuries under C/L occurred whilst the public were involved in SRA (HSE, 1997: p. 6). 18% of *all* major injuries to the public at a workplace occurred whilst involved in SRA (HSE, 1997: p. 6). It is disturbing to see that major injuries to the public under C/L have "more than doubled in the five year period [to 1995/96]" (HSE, 1997: p. 6). This may reflect improved reporting, but there is little evidence for this assertion.

Consumers, it would appear, rarely consider safety as a determining factor in their purchasing decisions until, that is, they are confronted by evidence of a clear risk (Anderson, 1995). A possible reason for this is the difficulty of assessing what constitutes a safe environment. In general we leave it to trust and our belief in there being established norms of safety, which we expect to be followed. So, when serious avoidable injuries do occur as a result of neglect, particularly to vulnerable groups (e.g. children) society often demands swift action, which can result in upheaval and great

**Table 1:   Sports and Recreation Industry —
Major injuries to public and employees
in the five-year period to 1995/1996**

	major injuries to:	**public**	**employees**
	no. of injuries :	2,592	465
% resulted from:			
a slip or trip		56%	38%
fall from a height		33%	28%
injuries involving a fracture		95%	81%
being struck by a moving object		—	8%
no. of equestrian sports injuries		391	109

Source: (HSE, 1997 p. 7-8; p. 13)

inconvenience and cost to consumers and the leisure sector (cf. Football Stadia). Changes to safety practice, all too often follow from such adverse circumstances. Our system of safety at leisure venues is borne out of such a history (Everton, 1996). Safety at sports grounds, hotels, cinemas and activity centres all illustrate this pattern of development.

How safety is valued by a consumer society is all too often demonstrated by how it arrives at its safety regulations, whether in the aftermath of an accident or in the normal course of its legislative process. The latter route is more difficult for Governments as such action will be regarded as unnecessary (in the absence of accidents) and over regulating businesses. The English experience is that the former route all too often precedes specific legislation (e.g. Outdoor Activity Centre legislation).

The leisure sector, by its very nature, exposes consumers to a greater degree of risk than most other forms of consumption and its significance increases by the year. The sector has been subject to a tidal wave of legislation since the Fire Precautions Act 1971 and, more recently, a greater willingness of the authorities and the public to take matters to both the criminal and civil courts. This paper identifies the extent to which intervention has taken place, the role of safety agencies and the effect this has had on the leisure sector and consumers. It considers whether self regulation and free market regulation are appropriate as a course of action and how this compares with direct government intervention, which has more recently been challenged by the concept of deregulation.

One of the features that distinguishes present safety legislation for the leisure sector is its piecemeal development. Robens in 1972 identified piecemeal development as a major defect in the system and militating against safety awareness (Barrett and Howells, 1993). Unfortunately, safety is not only addressed by the Health and Safety at Work Act 1974 (HSWA 1974) and the Fire Precautions Act 1971 (FPA 71) — both of whose main emphasis is the workplace, and not the consumer — but by a mass of legislation which, pieced together, forms an unattractive mosaic to those seeking guidance on the law. The situation is compounded by the variety of bodies which have been entrusted with overseeing such legislation. Any examination of a safety culture in a consumer society must, firstly, identify the relevant organisations and the laws which govern it.

Organisations

The organisations referred to here are responsible for the State's intervention on behalf of the public. As such this involves Public law and prosecution can result. Civil liability is distinct from this and will be referred to separately. There are three main bodies producing safety legislation:

*   The European Union (Directorates General V and X1) e.g. produced Directive on product liability (85/374/EEC);

*   The United Kingdom Parliament e.g. produced HSWA 1974; and

*   (Other) bodies delegated to introduce regulations, in particular Government Ministers and local Authorities (bye-laws), under the authority of an existing Act and which is recorded as a statutory instrument e.g. Reporting of Injuries, Diseases and Dangerous Occurrences Regulations (RIDDOR) 1995.

Very often major changes to safety regulations have been made without Parliamentary debate and both consumers and businesses are unsure as to where the law has come from. Since the Single European Act 1986, European Directives have become a particularly important source of Health and Safety law as the European Union seeks harmony in this area. Such legislation only requires majority, not unanimous, support to be enacted.

To make matters more confusing there is no one Government Department responsible for safety, and responsibilities can be traced to:

*   Home Office (Police and Fire Services);

*   Department of Trade and Industry (Consumer safety);

*   Department for Education and Employment;

*   Department for Culture, Media and Sport (Football Licensing Authority);

*   The Lord Chancellors Department (English Legal system); and the Department of the Environment, Transport and the Regions (responsible for the HSE; HSC and The Environmental Agency).

It is almost easier to refer to those Departments which do not have such a responsibility! Clearly each of these departments will have a different perspective on safety depending on the main focus of its work. This shared interest in safety results in confusion for the consumer and the leisure industry.

In Wales many of these departments come under the control of the Welsh Office and some benefits may arise as a result.

Local Government has its own safety labyrinth and which can do little to make matters easier. Product safety (e.g. under the Consumer Protection Act 1987) is dealt with by the Trading Standards Officers at County and Metropolitan District level. Workplace safety and Food hygiene is the responsibility of Environmental Health Officers at District Council and Metropolitan District level, such work is mainly focused on commercial leisure operations (the Health and Safety Executive cover, in the main, public provision of leisure). Licensing of Theatres, Cinemas, Public Entertainment, and Indoor Sports is also covered by the Licensing section, if they have one, of the Local and Metropolitan District Councils. Planning and Building Regulations are also covered by Local and Metropolitan District Councils typically within a Planning Department. Care of children under 8 is covered by County and Metropolitan District Council Social Services. Sports Ground Certificates are covered by Metropolitan District Councils and County Councils, the department responsible varies from one authority to another.

Licensing of establishments selling alcohol is covered by the licensing Justices at the Magistrates Court. A major consideration of granting such a licence is safety.

The local Police are also involved in the process of granting licenses (e.g. Public Entertainments licence and Alcohol licenses), the Fire Service is responsible for Fire Safety at all establishments and for granting certificates to relevant premises (e.g. hotels and boarding houses accommodating six or more people).

The two major bodies associated with safety are the Health and Safety Commission (HSC) and Health and Safety Executive (HSE). They were created under s.10 of The HSWA 1974. The distinction between the two is fairly clear — the Commission has responsibility for developing the objectives of the act, for instance through training, research and proposing new regulations; the Executive is mainly concerned with the enforcement of the Act and its regulations through its inspectorate (Barrett and Howells, 1993). However, for historical reasons, some of its work is carried out by Local Authorities (see above), the Health and Safety (Enforcing Authority) Regulations 1989 governs the exact details. A more recent development has been the delegation of its work to private organisations — so that Tourism Quality Services Ltd is the Licensing Authority for Activity Centres providing adventure activities for Young Persons (Donne, 1996).

It is somewhat ironic that the Robens Committee Report (Robens, 1972) identified, amongst other reasons, the "fragmentation of administrative jurisdictions" as mitigating against safety awareness and resulted in apathy, the most important single reason for accidents (Barrett and Howells, 1993: p. 40). The present position of mixed responsibility for safety does little to encourage the public and businesses to regard the overseeing of safety as other than confusion. The legislation covering leisure safety compounds the situation by offering little clarity.

Legislation (Public law only)

The main acts affecting the leisure sector are:
   Activity Centres (Safety of Young Persons) Act 1995
   Buildings Act 1984
   Children's Act 1989 (Children under 8 yrs old)
   Cinematograph Acts 1909, 1952, 1982, 1985
   Consumer Protection Act 1987 (Safety of goods)
   Employment of Children Act 1933, 1969
   Environmental Protection Act 1990
   Fire Precautions Act 1971
   Fire Safety and Safety of Places of Sport Act 1987
   Food Safety Act 1990
   Health and Safety at Work Act 1974 [Plus Regulations relating to First Aid
       (1981); Hazardous Substances (1994)]; Risk Assessment (1992);
       Information at work (1989); Safety Representatives (1977); Reporting
       of Accidents and Diseases (1995);
   Licensing Acts 1964, 1988 (Alcohol)
   Local Government (Miscellaneous Powers) Act 1976 (Fairgrounds)
   Local Government (Miscellaneous Provisions) Act 1982 (Entertainments'
       Licensing)
   Private Place of Entertainment Act 1967
   Safety of Sports Grounds Act 1975
   Sporting Events (Control of Alcohol etc) Act 1985
   Theatre Act 1968
   Town and Country Planning Act 1990 (Planning Permission)

The above legislation can be divided into those Acts which require an organisation to regularly prove that it has reached a pre determined standard in order to operate and those which require self regulation. The Acts also vary in their focus, some are focused upon the protection of workers, some on consumers and others attempt to do both by way of reference to the workplace. The Consumer Protection Act 1987 and Food Safety Act 1990, in contrast with the HSWA 1974, are focused on protecting the consumer from dangerous goods and food irrespective of location or organisation making the sale. Fire protection is also focused on workplace protection (with the exception of accommodation) and certificates are only required when the premises are designated, the great majority of leisure premises are not subject to regular inspection. It is not surprising, therefore, to find that only when accidents occur in the leisure sector, and inspections are carried out, that serious faults are found and further legislation proposed. Major Football grounds were already covered by the HSWA 1974 and the FPA 71 and yet they now also need a Sports Ground Certificate to ensure safety is maintained.

Guidance on leisure safety is plentiful and bodies such as HSE; The Institute of Leisure and Amenity Management; The Sports Councils; The Institute of Sport and Recreation Management and Government Departments all produce exhaustive guidance in these areas, identifying good practice based upon a wealth of detailed research. Fairgrounds and Amusement Parks; Swimming Pools; Golf Courses; Activity Centres; Sports Grounds; Crowd Control; and Riding Centres are all examples of activities which have been analysed and provided with clear safety documentation. The HSE also operates regional offices, computer databases, a monthly magazine, bulletins and even a fax response system. In short no one should complain that a system of self regulation has been hampered by a lack of assistance from the authorities and trade organisations.

All commercial Activity Centres were covered by the HSWA 1974 prior to the Lyme Bay canoeing tragedy in March 1993, yet there had been "little contact" by HSE and local authority inspectors as activity centre standards "were considered to be acceptable" (HSE, 1996: p. 4). Yet there is evidence of clear abuse prior to the present system of licensing (Trotter, 1994). The 1996 *Report into safety at outdoor activity centres* (HSE 1996) reveals that in 1994, a year after the Lyme Bay tragedy, there were still centres without: a Safety Policy (40%), formalised Risk Assessment (17%), a nominated Health and Safety representative (9%), instructor training (21%) and a formalised emergency procedures (7%). These statistics improved dramatically for the follow up visit (a year later), but demonstrate that despite Lyme Bay, the national publicity, the clear Health and Safety legislation and available guidance the system of self regulation was still not wholly effective. Unfortunately, the present system of legislation has very much a band aid feel to it. As problems arise so direct action is taken but with the result that more and more agencies and regulations are involved in the process. The Consumer Association in considering Playgrounds (*Which?* July 1994), Crowd Safety (*Which?* March 1995) and Leisure Park Safety (*Which?* August 1994) identify weaknesses in the present system of regulation which, it believes, continues to put the public at risk.

In its report on Transport safety (*Which?* July 1996) the Consumer Association reveals a clear pattern of major accidents, involving air, sea and coach transport followed by a reluctance, on the part of the authorities to 'make changes that put the UK at a commercial disadvantage' (*Which?* July 1996: p. 12). This does reveal one of the major problems of ensuring safety for the consumer, it is often perceived by leisure businesses and others as unnecessary interference by the State and likely to cause commercial hardship. Simmonds (1996) and Jenkins (1996) both highlight the enthusiasm of leisure organisations to move towards deregulation. But, Jenkins highlights the fact that the St Albans Centre, Lyme Regis, "had been visited by the British Activity Holiday Association (voluntary body) yet after inspection was found to be unsafe" (Jenkins, 1996: p. 25). The Conservative

Government introduced the Deregulation and Contracting Out Act in 1994 with the intention of removing unnecessary restrictions for business and The Fire Safety and Safety at Sports Grounds Act 1987 removed various classes of premises needing Fire Certificates. There is clearly a belief that safety regulations are against business interests. The privatisation of much of the organisation within the leisure sector will have added to the pressure on Governments to be sensitive to business concerns.

Another problem with self regulation is the poor legal protection given to leisure staff who wish to rectify unsafe practices by whistleblowing. Both the Consumer Association (*Which?* April 1996) and Public Concern at Work (Nolan, 1996) have identified this area as preventing information coming out about unsafe practices from employees concerned about their job security. At present the law offers only limited protection (Employment Rights Act 1996, s. 44) to those employees who speak out; the leisure sector has a high turnover of staff and is not recognised for its job security nor its Union membership. The concern, not to rock the boat, would certainly continue even with greater legal protection, and clearly many unsafe practices would carry on even though known to staff. Research has also revealed that many staff do not report incidents as they feel that "they may incriminate themselves or feel a report would be pointless" (Wojtas, 1997).

The message that one has of safety in the leisure sector is of a well intentioned approach but which has fallen short of the ideals of the Robens Committee. It noted that "...safety is mainly a matter of the day-to-day attitudes and reactions of the individual". In order to foster this it recommended the "need [for] a more effectively self-regulating system". (Barrett and Howells, 1993: pp. 40-41). Unfortunately, it would seem almost inevitable that although self regulation works for the majority of organisations and consumers it allows rogue practices to develop which will, inevitably lead to accidents and injury. What indications are there that the public would be willing to see more action to prevent accidents? Resort to Civil action suggests there is less acceptance by the public of poor practice and that the courts are prepared to find liability in the absence of Government intervention.

Civil remedies

The law, as such, has changed little in its direction over the last twenty five years. The main remedies are actions for Breach of Contract, Negligence and, in some instances, Breach of Statutory duty.
The main supporting legislation is:

- The Consumer Protection Act 1987 (remedy for dangerous goods);
- Supply of Goods and services Act 1982 (need for care and skill in contractual relationships);
- Occupiers Liability Acts (1957 and 1984) — safe premises;
- Unfair Contract Terms Act 1977. Exclusion of terms relating to death and personal injury.

The great difference, though, between now and the 1970s is the willingness of the injured to take matters to the Courts. This is clearly relevant as to whether we, as a society, demand safe practices and are no longer prepared to accept accidents as part of modern life. This is well illustrated by the Police Officers who successfully sued their employer for psychological injuries resulting from the negligence at Hillsborough (Frost and others v Chief Constable of South Yorkshire *The Times* 6 November 1996), the case is also of significance in that the Appeal Court confirmed that mental and physical injuries should be treated no differently from one another. Also in 1996 Ben Smoldon, a 17 year old rugby player, successfully sued an amateur referee for injuries resulting from negligent supervision of a game (Smoldon v Whitworth and Nolan *The Times* April 23 1996). Football players have succeeded in suing one another for injuries on the field (Condon v Bassi 1985 2 AllER 453), professional players owing a greater duty of care than amateurs, to other players. Gardiner (1993) warns coaches of sports that "it is not enough, at least in sports where injuries might occur, for coaches to plead ignorance or to attempt to argue that coaching is a subjective art and that they cannot be blamed for unfortunate consequences" (p. 13). Anderson (1995) identified high expectations of safety at Sport Courses from parent groups ("safety at all costs": p. 154) and a willingness of injured parties to resort to law (p. 160). Clancy (1995) and Woodhouse (1993), as lawyers, recognise the increased willingness of the public to resort to law after sustaining sporting injury. Utley (1996), as a coach and former rugby international, acknowledges the implications of such court actions. The Courts have been loathe to accept defences that the Plaintiff was involved in a risky activity and should accept the risk of possible injury (the volenti rule). All the above points to a public which feels it has a right to safety and expects others to act responsibly and be subject to scrutiny.

Conclusion

It would appear that the public have a high expectation of safety at leisure venues, that it is difficult for them to assess such venues and so have to put their faith in the professionalism of, an often unknown organisation. Unfortunately, the threat of civil action alone is not sufficient to secure safe practice (Barrett and Howells, 1993: p. 2) and since the middle of the nineteenth century Parliament has imposed criminal liabilities to protect those in the workplace environment. The free market approach to safety has few supporters, least of all because it requires full knowledge on the part of the consumer. The present system puts a great deal of trust in those providing leisure facilities, the trust that they will put safety centre stage of their operations, without regard to time and cost, and impose appropriate standards. As a society we recognise the need to have a driving licence and each year to subject the majority of cars to tests, yet, until relatively recently sports grounds, activity centres, hotels and children's care facilities could operate without regular inspection. That has changed, but only because tragedies had to take place first. In these areas a safety culture may have existed but, unfortunately, not to a degree that prevented these accidents. If we rely on promoting a leisure culture through self regulation it must provide, ultimately, the same if not better results than a regulated system. Making sure that the majority of businesses are safe is not good enough as a benchmark for success.

Amongst the public, there exists a safety culture in its expectations and a willingness to be inconvenienced if safety is secured. We are clearly better informed about safety issues through education, the media and the work of safety organisations and this applies not only to the public but to businesses. However, like environmental issues, change only seems to come about when it is either linked to selling the product or being subject to regular scrutiny. Certificates and licenses, although bureaucratic offer the best guarantees that standards are in place.

There are already many providers of leisure activities who need to have a licence or certificate in order to operate, and we have accepted time after time that the Health and Safety philosophy of Robens has clear weaknesses. In spite of that, deregulation has emerged as a fashionable concept in the free market environment that we now live in, it is associated with freedom of the individual. Deregulation, though, can also remove the freedom of the public to have safe regulated environments. It may be a good time, as we approach the twenty fifth anniversary of the HSWA 1974, to review all organised leisure activities and accept that simply hoping for a safety culture in the leisure sector may be a bridge too far.

References

Anderson, J. (1995) 'Safety at their leisure — A study of Youth Sport Courses', in L. Lawrence, E. Murdoch and S. Parker (eds) *Professional and development issues in leisure, sport and education* (LSA Publication No. 56). Eastbourne: Leisure Studies Association, pp. 147-165.

Barrett, B. and Howells, R. (1993) *Health and safety law*. London: Pitman.

Clancy, R (1995) 'Judo mats, climbing walls, trampolines and pole vaulters', *Sport and the Law Journal* Vol. 3: pp. 28-31.

Donne, K. (1996) 'Licensing ours', *The Leisure Manager* August/September: pp. 36-37.

East Midlands Council for Sport and Recreation (1995) *Safety and Risk in the Countryside Nottingham*. In house publication.

Everton, R. (1996) 'Fire safety law — retrospect and prospect', *Fire Prevention* 294 November: pp. 15-17.

Gardiner, J. (1993) 'Should coaches take care?', *Sport and the Law Journal* Vol. 1 pp. 11-13.

HSE (1994) 'Injuries to members of the public occurring in Swimming Pools 1993/94'. Unpublished. Statistical Unit. Health and Safety Executive, Bootle.

—— (1996) *A report into safety at outdoor activity centres*. London: HMSO.

—— (1997) 'Key Fact sheet on injuries within The Consumer/Leisure service Industry reported to Local Authorities 1991/92 to 1995/96'. Operations Unit. HSE. Bootle. Unpublished.

Jenkins, I. (1996) 'Out and about', *Leisure Management* February: pp. 24-25.

Nolan (1996) *Second Report of the Committee on Standards in Public Life* p. 21 Cm 3270. London: HMSO.

Office for National Statistics (ONS) (1997) 'Deaths from non transport accidents ... 1992-1995' (Table 12), *Mortality Statistics Injury and Poisoning 1997*. London: HMSO.

Robens (1972) *Robens Committee Report on Safety and Health at Work Cm 5034*. London: HMSO.

Simmonds, B (1996) 'Slow progress', *Leisure Management* June: pp. 22-23.

Trotter, S (1994) 'Activity holidays and the law', *New Law Journal* April 1: pp. 454-455.

Utley, R. (1996) 'A game referees can only lose', *Guardian* Newspaper 19 April: p. 21.

Which? (July 1994) 'Danger in the playground', Consumer Association London: pp. 26 -29.

—— (August 1994) 'Thrills not spills', Consumer Association London: pp. 30-34.

—— (March 1995) 'Safety in numbers?', Consumer Association London: pp. 36-39.

—— (April 1996) 'Whistleblowing', Consumer Association London: pp. 24-25.

—— (July 1996) 'When disaster strikes...', Consumer Association London: pp. 8-12.

Wojtas, O. (1997) 'Train lines kept safe from prying eyes', *The Times Higher* September 5: p. 8.

Woodhouse (1993) 'Role of the lawyer in sport today', *Sport and the Law Journal* Vol. 1: pp. 1-3.

The Search for a Level Playing Field: Planning and Sports Stadia Developments

Sarah McIntosh and Fiona Simpson

Edinburgh College of Art / Heriot Watt University / Scottish Agricultural College

Introduction

The Taylor Report (1991) instigated a surge in activity in developing stadia and sports grounds in the UK (Harcup, 1994). In addition, planning authorities and development corporations have increasingly looked to sports facilities (including stadia) as a catalyst for urban regeneration. Sports stadia have often been viewed as a panacea for depressed areas, acting as flagship projects within civic marketing strategies (Ragas *et al.*, 1987, Blount, 1990). More recently the literature has begun to emphasise the necessity of taking a more measured and cautious response to such an opportunity (Pritchard, 1994). In short, whilst this has become an issue of growing relevance for planners, at the same time there has been an increasing recognition of the controversial and complex nature of such developments.

This paper explores the role of local planning authorities within the process of the development of sports stadia in the UK. The research is based on data gathered by Fuller Peiser, Property Consultants identifying development activity in England and Wales since 1985 (estimated 75% coverage), covering a wide range of sports. The key aim of the research was to take existing literature on the subject a step further through linking quantitative research, which has characterised the planning literature on the subject, with more qualitative aspects and experiences. In doing so, the paper draws conclusions from the detailed exploration of a number of case studies in the UK. Aspects of good practice are highlighted, the issues and problems confronting the planning system are discussed and suggestions are made as to improved definition of the role of communities, developers and other stakeholders within the process.

The issues

In general the development of new stadia would appear to have been supported, at least in principle, by the planning system over recent years. The implications for land use planning have been documented in a broad range of literature, ranging from planning guidance and practical design guides to sociological research and detailed economic cost-benefit analysis. In identifying an appropriate framework for analysing developments to date, two main strands of the literature can be identified:

1. Process orientated issues

The role of the planning authority is discussed in the literature. The proactive approach to stadia development by planning authorities is often cited, with guidance advocating close co-operation between planning authorities and teams / stadia developers in identifying new sites. Some of the literature criticises central government guidance for not providing more tangible strategic guidance in the form of targets and co-ordination of national resources. This aspect is also linked to discussions about assessing supply and demand for new stadia, with Pritchard (1994), for example, predicting oversupply of facilities in the future resulting in their under use, if the established trend in levels of provision is maintained. Central government policy and guidance is set out in Planning Policy Guideline (PPG) No. 17 (England and Wales), and National Planning Policy Guideline (NPPG) No. 11 "Sport, Physical Recreation and Open Space" (Scotland), and at the local level through structure and local plan coverage.

PPG No. 17 sets out the recommended approach for the planning system to respond to both the implications of the Taylor Report, and the continuing increase in demand for sports facilities on a more general level. This guidance for England and Wales advocates a relatively positive approach to sports development, with an emphasis on supporting provision of new facilities as well as maintaining a focus on control through the planning system. The guidance suggests a range of development criteria which would establish a development proposal on a favourable basis, including the use of derelict land, locating on the urban fringe, use of sites near noise generators etc. In short, PPG17 supports sport and recreation as a legitimate land use issue in its own right (Sports Council for Wales, 1993) and emphasises the role of planning in providing opportunities for sport, and ensuring these opportunities are available to everyone.

The role of the community is important, including issues such as the enforcement of public order, views of supporters on relocation, and local opposition to new sites. A more sociologically oriented area of research, maps the external effects of football stadia in terms of their spatial context and surrounding land use with, perhaps predictably, a correlation between proximity to stadia and perceived nuisance generated having been noted (Bale, 1990; Mason and Moncrieff, 1993). The cultural associations of football club locations with traditional areas of support is a further important factor for consideration, particularly due to the potential stadia have for reinforcing community identity. Shared use as a means of boosting community benefit is also of interest.

The role of local politics is closely linked to social and cultural aspects of stadia construction, but nevertheless is distinctive, given the influence it has over the final outcomes of decision making process. The degree of local authority intervention is often highly influential within the stadia development process. At the same time, personalities of councillors and local pressure groups have an important role to play. This aspect often links closely with the wider issue of economic gain, particularly in areas of industrial decline and restructuring. Some particularly interesting case studies have arisen along these lines in the UK since the 1980s.

The role of prospective developers lends a specifically commercial orientated dimension to the discussion. The financial implications and economic viability of stadia development activity are a complex field alone, with options including ancillary developments, debentures, shares, property projects, new board members, selling players and funding from the Football Trust. There have been calls for greater government support in this field, particularly for smaller football clubs (Black and Lloyd, 1994). The availability of national lottery funding adds a further dimension to this issue, as well as European Funding programmes such as ERDF RECHAR etc. Assessing market demand, the underestimation of structural costs and income potential of stadia are further issues for exploration under this category with the use of cost benefit analysis and the multiplier principle as elements of financial appraisals of stadia developments.

2. Development specific / output issues

The interaction of the process orientated elements present a dynamic relationship which is further influenced by a range of more development specific but nevertheless fundamental aspects of stadia development. These issues are often related to the location of the site, and are encountered through the statutory requirements of the planning process. They include development characteristics; location; transportation issues; physical / environmental impacts; economic impacts; role of redundant stadia; and health and safety criteria.

Research Questions

The above themes have been investigated further through research questions being applied to the case studies. The idea inferred by the data as a whole, that clubs expect to be treated as a special case in negotiations with planners, is important in considering the process itself. The RTPI study also underlined a lack of co-operation between clubs and developers within the planning process (RTPI, 1996). Initial examination of the cases identified a recurring lack of detailed information within planning applications, and a strong need for clubs to become more involved in the earlier stages of development planning to ensure inclusion of their development options prior to applying for permission. The degree to which these problems could be seen as attributable to the clubs or the planning system has therefore been assessed, with potential for resolving this conflict being explored through examples of good practice.

Case Study Findings

Category 1 — Local authority as a catalyst for development.

It could be argued that there will always be a major role for local authorities in the development of sports stadia. In the case of the Kirklees MacAlpine Stadium, in Huddersfield, the local authority set up a partnership approach with the sports clubs through establishing a joint venture company to develop the stadium. The local authority was involved at the very beginning from site selection and the identification of the preferred site through to its development and eventual management. Huddersfield Town Football Club and Huddersfield Rugby League Club were both involved, and the fact that there were two different sports included gave added leverage to obtain further grants and finance. Although local authority involvement provided an added impetus for the clubs to work together, the clubs had already been co-operating before the new stadium was built.

Huddersfield Town Football Club had been seeking to relocate from their previous ground at Leeds Road since 1985 but any successful scheme was dependent on them achieving a good price for the sale of their ground. The club had been refused planning permission for food retailing on their site which they hoped would realise £6 million. At this time it seemed that Kirklees Metropolitan Council were not sympathetic to the ambitions of the football club. A change in management at Huddersfield Town encouraged a different approach of trying to work with Kirklees Metropolitan Council to help meet the council's aspirations for the regeneration of Huddersfield. The Council, and in particular the council chairman John Harman, became convinced that the successful development of a multi-use sports stadium would provide a major boost to Huddersfield.

A site was identified only 300 metres from the existing ground and approximately 1 km from the town centre. The land was allocated as an employment site in the local plan. It was vacant and in the ownership of the council; part of it had formerly been a chemical works. Although the allocation of the site had the support of the local authority, it was a departure from the approved Development Plan. It therefore had to be forwarded to the Department of the Environment for their approval. This was a frustrating procedure and added to the initial planning timetable. The planning arguments in favour of the development included the potential reuse of contaminated vacant land, the potential employment opportunities and the evidence that there were no other suitable sites, in particular flat sites, in the area. In the mean time Kirklees Metropolitan Council's shopping policy had identified the former ground at Leeds Road as appropriate for non food retail.

Although the role of the local authority was a major factor in the development process it should also be noted that the stadium development appears to have been successful for a number of other reasons, particularly strong management / leadership, and fortunate timing.

Another example of local authority involvement in the planning for a sports stadium is in Edinburgh where a working group of officers was set up in consultation with Heart of Midlothian and Hibernian Football Clubs to review alternative sites for a football stadium for Edinburgh. The working group comprised officers from Lothian Regional Council, City of Edinburgh District Council, Midlothian District Council, West Lothian District Council and Lothian and Borders Police. While it would appear that the local authorities were taking a proactive role, the working party was only set up after the clubs had begun to actively search for alternative locations for stadia and Hearts had already submitted a planning application for a stadium and other uses, including a business park and housing, within the green belt to the west of Edinburgh.

For the purposes of the working party study it was agreed that initially the prime objective of the search should be to meet the needs of a football club as an operational requirement. An area of potential conflict was apparent even at this preliminary stage. Hearts had requested an element of offices within the stadium "partly for the Club's own use". While the working party accepted this as part of the assessment they also stated that it would be viewed against the land use policies of the local planning authorities. The working party was therefore looking solely for a site to accommodate a football stadium and was not taking into consideration any wider development or commercial issues.

The alternative sites were judged against four main criteria:
1) Road network and accessibility;
2) Availability of public transport;
3) Green belt or non green belt;
4) Regeneration potential.

The major conclusion was that there were no suitable sites in an urban location, i.e. inside the greenbelt, that would meet the requirements for a new football stadium. The major problem appeared to be finding a site large enough although the requirement for 60 acres could be questioned as this included room for 6000 car parking spaces.

Despite this study and a number of planning applications for developments including a football stadium, both clubs eventually decided to stay at their existing sites and have committed considerable investment to carry out improvement works. The involvement of the local authorities did not lead to the successful development of a new stadium notwithstanding it did clarify the issues involved and demonstrate that although the shortlisted sites were located in the green belt there would need to be careful justification for any such policy exception. Although it was not explicitly stated it was also implied that there was unlikely to be a case to justify ancillary development other than recreational / leisure related uses linked to a multi-use facility. The financial considerations of developing a new stadium were not taken into consideration.

Category 2 — Viability and use profile

Sunderland Football Club was chosen as a case study because of the involvement of Tyne and Wear Development Corporation, both as owners of the site and as the planning authority. In the light of the Taylor Report the Club commissioned an initial feasibility study which concluded that the introduction of all seated accommodation would reduce the capacity of Roker Park to an unacceptably low level and that the costs involved could not be justified.

Sunderland City Council accepted that the stadium at Roker Park was no longer suitable and undertook a review of suitable sites in consultation with Sunderland Football Club as part of the preparation of the unitary development plan. The site originally identified by the study was in a green-field, out of centre location adjacent to the A19. A planning application was submitted that included retailing, commercial leisure and an exhibition centre. While it was contrary to existing policy, Sunderland City Council also identified the potential economic benefits of such a development, in particular in competing with the Metro Centre and Newcastle City Centre. The major objection to the site was access from the A19 which was considered to be a very important trunk road by the Department of Transport. The site was near to the Nissan Car Plant who were concerned that traffic congestion could affect delivery times which were critical to their working programme. The application was referred to the Secretary of State for the Environment but before it was determined the site at Wearmouth Colliery became available.

This site had not been originally identified in the search for suitable stadium sites because it had been thought to be a long-life 'superpit'. Its status changed when the coal industry was rationalised and privatised in 1993\94. The site is now owned by the Development Corporation but the football stadium land will be sold to the Club on completion of the building works.

The planning process was complicated by the fact that the application was originally considered by City of Sunderland Council as agents for the UDC. The application then went on to the UDC before being called in by the Secretary of State. The council officials considered that the application was called in because of the local interests of the UDC rather than policy issues. The relationship between Sunderland City Council and Tyne and Wear Development Corporation was strained at times although the planning officials felt that they had to stand their ground to ensure the best possible development.

Although it is acknowledged that the Wearmouth site is a good location for a football stadium there were a number of planning issues to be addressed, in particular, access to the stadium and car parking considerations. These were among the issues dealt with in the Environmental Statement.

The involvement of the UDC has acted as a catalyst for the development and has smoothed the way for the development more in land ownership and financial terms rather than the planning process. For example it funded the cleaning up of the site and a new access road that also improved access to the adjacent industrial area. The development has had a positive impact on the regeneration of Sunderland by improving what could have been a potentially difficult site to develop. The former Roker site is to be used for housing which will provide environmental and social benefits for its surrounding area.

The UDC are promoting the remainder of the site for a multiplex cinema but this is competing with two other proposals including one in the city centre which in policy terms would be preferable. The football stadium may have made the site more attractive to development but it is still subject to wider planning policies.

The Reading Case Study presented different issues regarding viability and land use. The planning authority were aware, at an early stage, that Reading Football Club were looking to relocate because of operational problems at their existing site. The need was identified in the relevant Local Plans and a Planning Brief was prepared for South West Reading which included the stadium site and other areas for business and retail. The initial discussions were held with the Chief Executive and the Project Officer from the Recreation Department with the Planning Department only becoming involved at the pre-application stage. The key issues were:

* the amount of enabling retail development that was required to fund the development costs of treating the contaminated land;

* traffic implications;

* contaminated land.

Despite the apparent willingness of the local authority to accommodate the development and to even include it in the modifications to the local plan there were still major difficulties to overcome. The development required Traffic and Retail Impact Assessments and it had also to address the contaminated land, waste licence and ground water supply problems.

The planning authority accepted that retail development was required at the site to generate sufficient finance to fund the other elements of the scheme including the stadium and treating the contaminated land. There was the added benefit of carrying out improvements on the existing Elm Park ground which allowed the A33 Relief Road to be implemented in the area and also for affordable housing to be constructed on the stadium site. The A33 Relief Road was part of wider strategic proposals in the area. A major factor that influenced the planning decision was the corporate commitment from the Council to the need to replace the stadium.

The planning official considered that the scheme had provided benefits in terms of regeneration and was contributing a landmark for the area but that limited community facilities had been provided by the development. The planning department would have welcomed more advice on how to include more community use of the facility. It is interesting to note that they did not comment on the impact of the retail element of the scheme.

Category 3   Political and Community Involvement

Charlton Athletic Football Club is an extreme example of how the Club supporters can try to affect the future development proposals of a football club. The Club had been located at The Valley, Charlton, since the beginning of the century. Lack of finance available to fund the ground improvements eventually forced the Club to leave The Valley in 1985. The Club moved to Selhurst Park to share with Crystal Palace. This proved to be an expensive move for Charlton. The numbers of "home" spectators were dropping fast with a crowd of only 4,205 in 1987 despite being in the First Division. Selhurst Park was only seven miles from Charlton but difficult to get to on public transport and was very unpopular with the fans.

In the autumn of 1985 a petition was organised by the local paper to campaign for the Club to return to Charlton and, preferably, the Valley. New management considered alternative locations for a stadium within the Borough, the most likely location was the former industrial areas in the Blackwall Peninsula which, according to the Club, was very close to going through. The scheme was not considered viable because of the restricted alternative development potential of the Valley ground.

The Club, instead, sought to redevelop the Valley with a 25,000 all seater stadium, housing, offices and 24 hour bowling alley and function suites. Although this proposal had a reasonable degree of support within the Council, it was considered unacceptable in terms of its' impact on the local residents. Significant pressure was put on the planning authority by the fans. There was uproar when the Council refused planning permission for the development. The fans were so outraged by the Council for thwarting the Club's plan to return to the Valley that they set up a political party and stood in the local elections later that year. They polled 14,838 votes, 10.9% of the total, and the former chairman of the planning committee lost his seat. A scaled down version of the proposal did get planning permission but it required the signing of a Section 52 (now 106) and this was never completed.

In 1992 and 1993, planning permissions were granted for refurbishment of the North and South Stands, erection of a temporary West Stand and erection of a new East Stand which was also subject to a planning agreement which covered issues such as:

* control over non-football uses such as pop concerts
* provision of residents' parking
* liaison group with local residents, police and the Club
* street cleaning requirements
* hours of use of the hospitality suites

In 1997, approval was given for the construction of a new West Stand which will complete the major redevelopment proposals for the Valley, providing a total capacity for 20,000 spectators and on-site car parking for 245 cars.

Although the case study does not involve the relocation of a stadia, it does raise some interesting and relevant issues.

1. The Football Club's and, in particular, the fans' expectation that the need for a stadium for Charlton Athletic would justify any scale of development on the site.

2. The lack of understanding of the potential impacts on the surrounding land uses such as housing, especially as a result of the intensification of use and the change of use to activities other than football, by the Club and fans.

3. The restrictions placed on the Club by the land use designation in the Local Plan. The Club had never objected to the Local Plan, either the People's Plan in 1989, or the UDP that was approved in 1994.

4. The lack of discussions between the Club and the Council led to misunderstandings that could have been addressed constructively in the planning process. It may also have led to the successful relocation of the Club to the Blackwall Peninsular with far less disturbance of the surrounding community. The Club now has much improved links with the Council and the local community and has four community officers who are part-funded by the local authority and the PFA and run courses in local schools.

5. The experience of ground sharing by Charlton Athletic Football Club, not only with other football clubs but also London Broncos Rugby Club, has put them off the concept of sharing their playing facilities.

The case study of Airdrieonians Football Club's attempts to relocate from their Broomfield site and develop a new stadium was included because of the large number of objections the initial application received and the effect that this response had on the subsequent proposals.

The planning application that received the most objections was the proposal at Raebog Road, Glenmavis, which, ironically, appears to be the most remote from the built up area. Objections were received from 1,101 individuals highlighting the possible car parking problems and traffic congestion that the development would bring. Local residents were also worried regarding the anticipated anti-social behaviour of football supporters. Although there were a large number of objections, the major reason for refusal was that it was contrary to approved greenbelt policy in the Structure Plan.

It is interesting to note that despite a study carried out by consultants and funded by Lanarkshire Development Agency, Monklands District Council and the Football Club, four further planning applications were submitted on four different sites before a planning consent was given.

In contrast, the site that was finally approved is bounded mainly by residential properties and the Council received 220 individual letters and two petitions objecting to the planning application. A residents group was also set up to object to the scheme. 2,520 letters, and a petition, were received in support of the stadium. How the letters and petitions objecting to, and supporting, the schemes were taken into account will need to be explored further.

Category 4 — Policy implications for site selection

The Government recognised the implications the Taylor Report had on out-dated sports stadia and requested Local Planning Authorities to give sympathetic consideration to development proposals to upgrade and modernise stadia facilities. The definition of 'sympathetic consideration' is therefore the critical issue here, in particular the relevance of policy guidance in both the choice of location and also the treatment of likely impacts.

The Dewsbury Rugby League Football Club case study was selected because planning permission was granted despite the proposal being located in the green belt. It is also an example of a smaller scale development of more relevance to sports other than football. To comply with the latest requirement for professional Rugby League grounds it was accepted that the only viable option to the club was to sell its' existing site for development of a kind which would enable a new stadium complex to be constructed. Land would have to be acquired at a minimum cost for the scheme to be fulfilled. The existing site at Crown Flatt was subsequently sold for housing land.

The proposed new ground is on land that was formerly part of the Shaw Cross colliery and has been reclaimed and laid to grass but is of low agricultural quality. The land is owned by the local authority. The site is designated as part of the green belt conurbation core. The planning application to erect a stadium with grandstands, club rooms, spectator accommodation and car parking was greeted favourably by Kirklees Metropolitan Council and attracted only three letters of objection. One day before the application was to go before the planning sub-committee with a recommendation for approval it was called in by the Secretary of State under Section 77 because the development was contrary to the development plan.

Subsequently a public local inquiry was held and the Planning Inspector recommended refusal of the planning application The inspector concluded that the area of green belt subject to the planning application was particularly vulnerable because it was a narrow neck of open land and any building on this land would be more noticeable because of its' function of separation and intervention between large built up areas within the conurbation. He stated that the whole club complex would represent a substantial loss of grassed, open area.

From reading the Inspector's conclusions it would almost suggest that the fact that the local authority had been involved in the site selection process and owned the identified site had influenced the consideration of the planning application and counted against the proposed development. The Secretary of State disagreed with his Inspector's recommendation and subject to a number of conditions gave consent.

The Portsmouth Football Club was again a case study where the planning application was called in by the Secretary of State under Section 77. The search for a new site was initiated by Portsmouth Football Club who recognised that their existing site was too small and land locked. In addition they needed more income to be able to run the club and to compete effectively. The Planning Department helped to identify alternative sites which were subsequently assessed by consultants. The football club identified Farlington as the most appropriate site from the shortlist of six. The key issue in its assessment was traffic considerations. The search for suitable alternative sites was constrained by the requirement to provide 4500 carparking spaces and park and ride. In addition the site had to be attractive to enable development to be able to fund the stadium.

Extensive public consultation was undertaken including a leaflet being distributed to every household in the City under Neighbourhood Notification procedures in addition to the statutory Press Notices. 6,980 letters were received with a further 9,372 signatures to petitions. The report to the planning committee recommended refusal on grounds relating to retail impact, detrimental effect on the provisions of public playing fields, highway concerns and having regard to the above the proposal would not accord with the City Plan for the relocation of the Club.

The full City Council resolved to grant conditional outline planning application subject to the Secretary of State not wishing to call the application in for determination, which of course he did. Following a public inquiry the application was refused. It is interesting to note that one of the major reasons for refusal is the impact on nature conservation. It is acknowledged by the planning officials that the local planning authority had underestimated the environmental issues and did not even request an Environmental Impact Assessment. It could be argued that it was not even national planning policy that operated against the proposed development but nature conservation designations supported by European legislation.

Conclusions

In bringing together the findings from the case studies, a whole host of issues emerge. This paper has sought to outline the implications of the findings for local planning authorities, and as a result our conclusions relate to this aspect of the work alone. In addressing the implications for planners, therefore, four key issues can be identified:

- The interaction and consistency between planning guidance, policy and implementation
- The nature of planning — from regulating to enabling
- Planners as mediators of stakeholder concerns
- Planning and community involvement

The interaction and consistency between planning guidance, policy and implementation

The literature has put forward a critique of national policy making and guidance in its lack of strategic co-ordination of developments (Casely-Hayford, 1991). Black and Lloyd (1994) also highlighted that two thirds of Scottish football clubs felt that government support was inadequate. One of the most fundamental problems relates more to the interface of policy making and intervention, as well as being compounded by a lack of co-operation or at least understanding between the various tiers of authorities. As a result, the case studies highlight the inconsistencies which abound. National transport policy, for instance, and its aim of reducing road traffic, has often been in direct conflict with local authority requirements for car parking and road access provision. Whilst the construction of a new stadia is not an everyday or repeated process within a single local planning authority area, where it does occur the lack of guidance and almost inevitable lack of previous experience in those dealing with the application, lead to confusion and ad-hoc problem solving approaches. As a result, many of the developments became long and drawn out, encountering many pitfalls and require considerable extra effort on the part of all the stakeholders.

The experiences point towards greater interpretation of national policy as a guide for local decision making. A good practice guide, or Planning Advice Note (PAN) would perhaps be suitable vehicles for bridging the gap between policy and implementation. Whilst each stadium and its locality are of course unique, a number of issues were shared by the case studies, which could be addressed by a framework for guidance. Even just advising planners of the full range of issues and considerations involved in developing a stadia would represent a significant step forward in providing local authorities with a more informed basis for decision making.

The nature of planning — from regulating to enabling

The importance of the local authority as a catalyst for development has been reviewed through our research. Although their role is considered to be significant several of the case studies have highlighted the problems that can arise when a development is supported by the local authority, but not included as a policy within a development plan. The application can then be called in by the Secretary of State whose Inspector may place different emphasis on the issues that should be taken into consideration when determining the planning application. The importance of the Development Plan must therefore be emphasised but it is accepted that the required timescales to produce a fully consulted and approved development plan will not accord with what is often a much shorter timescale to develop a sports stadium. The development plan is also relevant when considering the development potential of the existing sports ground if the proposal involves relocation from an existing stadium. Sports clubs should ensure that the site is not restricted by any policies within the plan. This is particularly important when a new plan is being written or revised.

The study demonstrates the importance placed on the policy implications for site selection from the initial search for potential sites through to the justification of a specific planning application at a public inquiry. The acceptance that any development contrary to a development plan requires exceptional circumstances to be justified is an important issue to be considered throughout the site selection and planning process. This requires clear and realistic criteria for site selection to be identified and explained at the beginning of the process. These criteria should also be related to the objectives of the Club, fans, local community, local authorities and central government and the relevant potential funding bodies and institutions. The case studies identified a number of operational considerations that require to be researched further, including car parking, public transport, ground sharing, community access and facilities and access for the disabled.

As outlined in the discussion of the previous issue, planners have an essentially regulatory role to play in the development of a stadia. However, this role could be seen as having dominated negotiation between developers and authorities, and as a result has detracted from the symbiosis required to enable a development of this scale and complexity. Planners who viewed their role in a more positive and proactive light were ultimately more successful. It should be stressed that local authorities have little to gain from polarising interests in the name of regulation.

Planners as mediators of stakeholder concerns

The research has identified the high level of interest there has been in proposals for stadia development by sports clubs, property developers, local authorities, development agencies, central government, surrounding communities, and last but certainly not least the fans. We are still developing an understanding of the relationships and interaction between these different bodies and further discussion will be required particularly with the sports clubs themselves.

There is clearly a case for supporting the contention of the RTPI, that

...in most cases it would appear that plans are simply not consistent with policy and local plan criteria...few football club administrators understand the planning system, its purpose and objectives and see it as an obstacle to their plans. Football clubs would do well in the earliest stages to make planning officers their allies, not a source of confrontation. (RTPI, 1996: pp. 23-4)

The Kirklees case implies that this should not necessarily be the situation, demonstrating the advantages of working in partnership with a local authority in developing a sports facility. The Council had a financial interest in the development through being a partner in the joint venture company and was therefore more aware of the financial viability issues of the scheme. In contrast, although a working party of local authority officials was set up to investigate the potential for alternative sites for football stadia around Edinburgh, the study really only took into account the planning implications of such a development and therefore did not identify realistic or commercially attractive sites.

It has already been discussed that the use profile of any new development can influence the viability of the scheme. This was certainly taken into consideration at Reading where it was accepted that a certain amount of retail development was required to make the whole scheme viable. The local authority were also influenced by the fact that by relocating the club considerable improvements could be made in the town centre. The potential regeneration benefits were recognised in a number of the schemes, particularly where the development had taken place on derelict or contaminated land. As demonstrated in the Sunderland case study, it is important to recognise that these improvements could lead to additional pressure for development in the area. In short, planning for new stadia has many impacts on a whole variety of groups and interests, which must be acknowledged if an effective solution is to be found.

Planning and community involvement

The planning system is based on a process of community consultation and involvement which has traditionally assumed a geographical focus, as a result of the spatially defined nature of its remit. The example of stadia development could be viewed as transcending preconceived ideas of the meaning of community, relating not only to the locality where the stadium is located, but also to the wider population of the town or city, as well as to the fans and supporters. The latter may be geographically dispersed, but nevertheless form a crucial interest group within the process. This cultural aspect in defining community should be recognised within the planning process, as often highlighted at the political level of decision making at the local level (as in the case of Dewsbury RLFC, for example). Despite this, "many communities end up at loggerheads with their famous neighbour" (RTPI, 1996: p. 24).

In addition, however, local views are crucially important. Where a stadium development is called in at the national level, as is often the case, or where it is a central part within an urban regeneration strategy, the local dimension can often give way to wider principles and objectives. In short, community involvement within the process must be recognised by the planning system as being complex, where it relates to developments which have the potential to alter perceptions of identity and local character unrecognisably. Brunner, summarises the overriding and often not strictly logical or reasonable nature of community concerns:

> The story of the Valley, demonstrates the loyalty of football fans, not simply to the club, but also to the stadium it plays in. Yet the Valley's value lies in its emotional ties rather than its merits as a venue for football. (1990: p. 44)

Clearly planning must assume a mediating role in such cases, essentially focusing on statutory decision making frameworks and requirements, but at the same time becoming sensitive to often irrational and emotional views.

Planning should recognise that redeveloping, relocating or even constructing a brand new stadium goes beyond traditional aspects of spatial, economic and social considerations, having potentially far reaching cultural impacts.

References

Bale, J. (1990) 'In the shadow of the stadium: Football grounds as urban nuisances', *Geography* No. 75: pp. 325-340.

Black, J. S. and Lloyd, M. G. (1994) 'Football stadia developments: Land use policy and planning controls', *Town Planning Review*, Vol. 65, No.1 (January): pp.1-18.

Blount, K. (1989) 'Sheffield's fast footwork', *Municipal Journal* (6 October): pp. 26-27.

Brunner, C. (1990) 'Grounds for improvement', *Leisure Management*, Vol. 10, No.6: pp. 44-52.

Casely-Hayford, M. (1991) 'No time for leisurely pace', *Planning*, No.940 (October): pp. 16.

Department of the Environment (1991) *Planning policy guidance: Planning and sport.* London: DoE.

Harcup, T. (1994) 'Council and clubs are premier partners', *Municipal Journal*, No. 25 (June): pp. 38-39.

Mason C., and Moncrieff, A. (1993) 'The effect of relocation on the externality fields of football stadia: The case of St. Johnstone Football Club', *Scottish Geographical Magazine* Vol. 109, No. 2 (September): pp. 96-105.

Pritchard, S. (1994) 'Sporting strategies', *Planning Week*, Vol. 2, No. 30 (28 July): pp. 16-17.

Ragas, Wade, R., *et al.* (1987) 'Louisiana Superdome: Public costs and benefits 1975-84', *Economic Development Quarterly*, Vol. 1, No. 3 (August): pp. 226-239.

RTPI (1996) *Planning and Football League Clubs*, in association with Stadium and Arena International. *Update Questionnaire Report.*

Scottish Office (1996) *Sport, physical recreation and open space.* NPPG No.11. Edinburgh: HMSO.

III

Leisure Capital, People and Places

The Experience of Unemployment and the Use of Leisure Capital

Francis Lobo

Edith Cowan University

Introduction

This paper deals with the leisure capital of unemployed senior citizens and their propensity to use it to cope with job loss. Data were derived through three-stage in-depth interviews with ten unemployed older persons. their spouses, and one off-spring. Interviews were held six months apart over the period of one year. This paper deals with three cases, one severely affected, one moderately affected and one minimally affected. It was found that unemployment affects people in diverse ways and that effect has an impact on how they utilise their leisure capital in and out of the home. The literature is examined on schemes using leisure to ameliorate the deprivations of unemployment and a question is raised to imply that positive use of leisure capital depends on the intensity of job loss impact. The names of participants stated in the paper are pseudonyms to protect their identity. The literature, which follows, examines some theoretical aspects of unemployment and leisure.

Unemployment and leisure

A vast literature exists on the impact of unemployment. Fryer (1995a) sums up by stating that the psychological consequences of unemployment are not homogenous. There is considerable variation from person to person amongst those affected in the severity of the psychological impact of unemployment. Some people's mental health is affected very badly, some people's moderately, and some people's hardly at all. For a minority psychological health appears to actually improve when they become unemployed. Two major but contrasting theories dominate unemployment theory. They are the deprivation and the personal agency approaches.

With the deprivation approach Jahoda (1979, 1984, 1986, 1992) argues that employment promotes well-being by providing people with a time structure, social contacts, a collective purpose, a sense of identity, and regular activity. These five 'categories of experience', as she terms them, are important adjuncts to the manifest consequence of earning a living. When people are unemployed they are deprived of access to these categories of experience and the manifest function of earning a living in the social institution of employment.

Fryer and Payne (1984) undertook a study of a small group of unemployed people who were experiencing material but not psychological deprivation by adopting a proactive stance towards unemployment. Ideas and concepts of their personal agency theory (1986) were further developed by Fryer (1995b) who summarised its assumptions on two grounds. Firstly, that people are socially embedded agents actively striving for purposeful self-determination, attempting to make sense of, initiate, influence and cope with events in line with personal values, goals and expectations of the future in a context of cultural norms, traditions and past experience. Secondly that, whilst personal agency is sometimes empowered in interaction with labour market social settings and systems, agency is frequently undermined, restricted and frustrated by formal and informal social forces. Commenting on the deprivation and personal agency approaches, Haworth (1997) concludes that Jahoda and Fryer both stress the importance for well-being of the psychological categories of experience. Jahoda stresses the importance of social institutions in facilitating access to these categories of experience, whilst Fryer points to the inhibitory influence which poverty, social arrangements and cultural practices can have on personal agency, thereby restricting access to positive categories of experience.

Leisure is regarded as a vital contributor to quality of life. Schemes for the unemployed have stimulated new participation and recruited back into sport a number of lapsed participants, but failed for most to sustain participation (Glyptis, 1994). For committed unemployed users, sports' leadership schemes did counteract many of the problems of unemployment (Kay, 1994). Studies of young unemployed adults by Evans and Haworth (1991), Haworth and Evans (1987) and Haworth and Ducker (1991) show that engagement in activity is associated with enhanced well-being, but it is less than that for a matched sample of employed people. However, not all types of leisure are able to provide access to the categories of experience.

Stebbins (1996) states that the new found free time of jobless people can provide opportunities for personal development in "serious leisure". He defined serious leisure (1992) as the steady pursuit of an amateur, hobbyist, or volunteer activity that captivates its participants with its many challenges and inherent complexity. Serious leisure is sufficiently substantial and interesting for the participant to find a career in the acquisition and expression of its special skills and knowledge. This kind of leisure stands in contrast to "casual" or "unserious" leisure, which poses many people few challenges, is much simpler in structure, and rarely requires a steady commitment to perform it well. According to Stebbins (1996: p.6), "there is a bewildering array of casual forms, among them strolling in the park, observing a fireworks display, going to a picnic, and taking an afternoon nap". The steady pursuit of leisure activities implies that participants have a reservoir of skills or leisure capital which they can draw from.

The term leisure capital arises from the work of Pierre Bourdieu (1985) who focused upon tastes and preferences in art but has general application to all forms of cultural activity and consumption such as sports, holidays, outdoor recreations, media, home decor, cars, clothes, drinks and other leisure-time activities. Leisure capital can take the forms of economic, cultural and symbolic goods and resources. Bourdieu studied the influence of social class upon leisure activity and used occupation as the main indicator. But what of those without paid occupations? For the unemployed leisure takes on different meanings. For some it is "enforced free time", others "...call it pressure" (Lobo, 1996a: p. 389).

Unemployed seniors in late career have built up stocks of leisure capital, which could be economic, social and cultural as well as physical assets. Economic capital could be savings, investments or even the possibility of having meagre discretionary expenditure for leisure activity. Social and cultural capital consist of social relationships, qualifications, attitudes and values, memberships in clubs and associations, activity skills, informal activities such as media consumption and home-based leisure. In addition, unemployed individuals might have assets such as golf clubs, bicycles, bats, racquets and reading material.

Schemes that have utilised leisure activities to provide access to categories of experience have accepted unemployed people as though the impact of job loss was homogenous. Current research (Fryer, 1995a) shows that it is not. Lobo (1996b) in a study sample of 71 participants found that job loss effects were severe (37 responses), moderate (14) and minimal (19). The question raised in this paper is: Does the degree of job loss affect an individual's capacity to draw on his or her leisure capital?

Methodology

Subjects, procedures and measures

A purposeful sample of ten information-rich cases (8 male and 2 female) between the ages of 50 and 55 years was selected. The unemployed persons, their spouses and one offspring were interviewed in-depth at three separate times during the year. The first interviews were held in the January-February period, the second in the June-July period and the third in the November-December period. This paper deals with three cases, one severely, one moderately, and one minimally affected and involved 27 in-depth interviews. Through open-ended questions eight categories of unemployment experience were examined: impact on self; job search; reduced income; family relationships and responsibilities; leisure and other activities at home; out-of-home leisure activities; personal resources; and external resources. This paper focuses on the impact on self, leisure and other activities in the home, and out-of-home leisure activities.

Participants were categorised as being severely, moderately and minimally affected. Those who were severely affected were deeply shocked with job loss and their behaviour was characterised by irritability, moodiness, withdrawal and cynicism over a long period of time. Participants who were shocked, stressed and concerned about their financial future soon after job loss, but as these concerns faded, adapted positively to unemployment in the short term, were categorised as being moderately affected. Minimally affected participants were those who did not experience shock after job loss, did not worry about it, and even thought of job loss as a relief.

Results

A severely affected case

Gerald Green was 51 years old with two grown children. His last job was as a glassworker in a window factory. His wife Beatrice, was non-employed and was a full-time housewife. The son Jim, aged 25, worked as a horticulturist on a university campus and did not live with his parents, but visited them weekly. At the time of the first interview, Gerald had been unemployed for twelve months.

In employment:

Gerald described himself as a happy, confident person with not many social friends. He looked forward to going to work because he "could talk to, relate to" workmates. Beatrice thought of her husband as "just a nice easy-going friendly person", "who enjoys being with his workmates". Jim, too, said his dad was "happier ... more confident, more easy going" when he was working.

Impact of unemployment:

Gerald was "shocked and stunned" when told he had lost his job just before leaving to work one day. He expressed anger and bitterness and between that time and the first interview, experienced depression, was irritable and moody, withdrawn and suffered from insomnia. In trying to dissipate his anger and frustration in the days soon after job termination, he worked in the garden and in doing so, damaged a nerve in his left and preferred arm, a disability which restricted future employment in a manual trade. Six months later Gerald had "mellowed a bit", but the impact had not worn off. The tension and anxiety seen at the first interview was still evident. His behaviour was volatile interspersed with periods of irritability, moodiness and withdrawal. He had become cynical, blaming the government who seemed "too busy worrying about silly piddly bloody stupid things". Twelve months later Gerald had "become a little more withdrawn, more anti-social, cynical ... ". By his own admission he had undergone "more or less a personality change".

Leisure and other activities at home:

Soon after unemployment, Gerald used his competent handyman skills to do jobs around the house, such as ripping the lawn, carpets, varnishing floors, painting doors, ceilings and outside the house, wall-papering the inside and brick paving a pathway at the back. He soon got fed up with home jobs and decided to attend night school to learn leadlighting. He knew how to cut glass and but didn't know how to lead it up and cement it. The leadlighting hobby kept him engrossed during the evenings for "two to three hours ... to take my mind off what's going on". It was an expensive hobby and Gerald had to make it pay for itself by selling the products he made. He did little to help Beatrice with domestic chores.

Six months later, Gerald had difficulty coping with unobligated time that unemployment imposed. He watched television, particularly sports, which drove Beatrice "up the wall". He was often bored and listless, but assisted his wife with house cleaning and peeling potatoes because the arthritis in her forearms and hands was getting worse. Gerald detested gardening, but only did it because he was asked to "dig a hole or get rid of branches". Besides giving little domestic help, Gerald developed an interest in reading. He went to the local library and brought books home. He preferred reading than "all day buggering about in the garden". The leadlighting hobby was discontinued because of the high cost of materials.

Twelve months later, Gerald's dislike of domestic tasks continued, but he unwillingly did more of them as Beatrice devised a day-to-day routine. He now did the house cleaning on Wednesdays when Beatrice went to doll-making classes. He also helped on Mondays, when cleaning was shared. He even helped with the washing, except in the morning, because he was "usually in bed". On Tuesdays, he shopped with Beatrice. A new hobby of making dolls' houses was occupying Gerald's mind. He had sold all the leadlighting tools, except the ones for cutting glass, because they would be required for the doll house windows. The dolls' house hobby was another way in which husband and wife could do things together, since Beatrice made all the dolls' clothing, bed linen, other accessories. Gerald's carpentry skills would come in useful in making dolls' furniture.

Out-of-home leisure activities:

Before unemployment Gerald's main leisure activity outside the house was playing golf. He was a member of a golf club and played weekly on Saturday mornings. After job loss he cancelled the membership because he couldn't afford it and being unemployed felt embarrassed in the company of employed people. He sold his golf clubs and lost contact with playing friends. Gerald substituted golf with voluntary activity of cleaning kennels at an animal haven close to home each Sunday morning. The activities at the animal haven stopped after six months and the social contact with a couple who were co-helpers ceased. On some weekends, Jim took his father fishing in his dinghy, just to take him out of the house. He noticed however, that dad wasn't able to sustain interest more than a couple of hours. Before unemployment they dined out occasionally. That had stopped altogether soon after job loss. Friendly neighbours of their age, who conversed frequently, borrowed tools, and waved when the Greens' car passed the house no longer did so after unemployment. Beatrice felt the social stigma of her husband's unemployment, was embarrassed by it, but did not hide the fact. Six months later, going to the city each Thursday and helping to restore Jim's home each Sunday were the new leisure activities outside the house. Twelve months later, these activities continued and they went out for lunch once in four weeks. According to Jim his father was sometimes enthusiastic, because he could do 'challenging' tasks and it was easier to get him to do harder jobs than easier ones.

A moderately affected case

Ross Timms aged 51 was married with two sons. He worked as an Area Manager for an electronics company for 18 years before he was retrenched. His wife Winnie worked as a legal secretary. Older son, Victor worked as an accountant, having recently graduated with a bachelor's degree. At the time of the first interview, Ross was unemployed for 14 months.

In employment:

Victor described his father as "very confident, pretty aggressive, outgoing and pretty dynamic". To Winnie, her husband was a workaholic, who kept going after 5.00pm, his average being 7.00pm and he went to the office on Saturdays and Sundays as well. She thought of him as being "terribly committed to work" and although he had time for the family, they "had to fit in with his work".

Impact of unemployment:

When Ross was made redundant, he felt "a little bit bitter, but also relieved". He also felt disheartened after all the effort and energy he put into the company. Winnie said "he was still very confident" when he lost his job and didn't think he would be out of work for long. However, three months after job loss, he got seriously ill, was near death, and when he recovered was happy just to be alive. His whole outlook on life had changed after the illness as job and money became immaterial to him. Six months later at the second interview, Ross felt that the company had treated him fairly and there was no hurt. There was no change to this attitude at the third interview.

Leisure and other activities at home:

When Ross was retrenched the family "went overboard" to see that Ross was kept busy with things like painting and redecorating the house. After his illness and as his health improved, he took on family responsibilities of house cleaning, redecorating, and gardening. He also helped with the cooking which he didn't do before. He maintained the routine of employment days by waking up at 5.30 each morning. Together with Winnie and Victor had breakfast at 6.00am. Ross would make the sandwiches for them before they went to work. He was much more involved with his sons, transporting one to university, and both to basketball training. At the second interview, he was more involved with household work and did it to be useful to Winnie so that she did not have to "do these sorts of things over the weekend". He found the company of his sons very interesting. In particular, the stories Victor brought home about what he was doing. Family life was strengthened. Twelve months later, Ross had taken over the cooking, washing and cleaning, things he had never done before. He had completed house maintenance jobs with "a sense of accomplishment". He spent a lot of time with his sons, got "a sense of satisfaction" working in the garden. He now described himself as "the happiest person under the sun" and was pleased to play an important role in family stability.

Out-of-home leisure activities:

After unemployment Ross cut off relations with work related friends. He did not have any other friends and did not belong to any clubs or associations. Six months later he engaged in voluntary work, driving elderly citizens to the library. He found the job satisfying. He was pleased to use his time effectively and help people in need, who were often lonely and wanted company. Twelve months later, with his health and confidence growing, Ross undertook a voluntary job, five days a week, driving handicapped young people, in wheelchairs, to work. When they finished their day's work, he picked them up and took them to their hostels or homes. The only other activity outside the home was walking each morning soon after his wife went to work.

A minimally affected case

David Patton was an electronic design engineer and was 55 years of age when retrenched. His wife Evelyn was employed as a registered nurse and daughter Jean, aged 22, worked as a receptionist. She lived with her fiancee away from home. At the time David was first interviewed, he was unemployed for 13 months. Evelyn was his second wife and was married to David for about a year. She therefore knew him as an unemployed person.

In employment:

Jean thought her father had "always been headstrong and independent" and "happy, very intelligent". David himself felt confident about his skills and abilities. Besides formal qualification in electronic design engineering, he had excellent skills as a pianist and in computing. In employment he played the piano once a week at a hotel.

Impact of unemployment:

Job loss came as a relief. David knew he could use his piano playing skills. He started playing the piano five nights a week at various hotels and "everything sort of dropped into place". He was happy, it was something he always wanted to do and "there was too much happening to feel depressed about anything". He was keen on a regular day job and registered at the local job centre seeking for work in his field. Six months later, David decided that getting back into electronics was "not the way to go anyway". He therefore made a choice of pursuing "more piano jobs" rather than trying to "get back into an ordinary job", so he was "concentrating a little more on teaching piano". Jean thought her father was more relaxed "doing what he wants to do" and Evelyn to said: "He looks more happy now". Twelve months later, David had given up look for a full-time job as he found it to be a "fruitless exercise". He applied to study at university "to get back into an intellectual stream of people, that you can debate with" something "which you don't get with musicians". David had side-stepped into piano playing as his main occupational role.

Leisure and other activities at home:

At the time of the first interviews Jean and Evelyn commented that David was never bored at home. He worked in the garden, on his computer, read books, played the piano, and was building the patio. Evelyn said that he always kept busy:

> He goes to his room and can spend hours, days, making and writing programmes which he likes... He reads books, plays the piano or does gardening. He just works. He does everything. He keeps himself busy. Actually, I don't see him idle at home.

Six months later jobs like repairing, gardening, fixing the car continued. His efforts focused on the computer, piano and health. Unemployment did not cause any psychological discomfort. With the piano and computer, David created his own challenges. The foregoing activities continued twelve months later with the addition of giving piano tuitions on some weekdays.

Out-of-home leisure activities:

Outside the house David shopped, played badminton and squash on separate days. Because of his piano playing, his social circle had increased, but social life with family friends and relatives was adversely affected when David played at nights. He found that "filling time" was "never a problem". After six and twelve months the foregoing activities of piano and sporting activities were sustained and the social circle increased. David thought his "liking of music on the one hand and science on the other" were the inner resources that kept him going.

Interpretation of data

The severely affected case:

Gerald Green dealt badly with unemployment. Formerly an easy-going friendly person, he became volatile, anti-social and cynical. His inflexibility to traditional gender role and work ethic attitudes was dysfunctional in unemployment. He failed to marshal the good handyman abilities he possessed for the many things that needed doing in the house. Beatrice's life would have been much happier if Gerald had done domestic chores, house repairs and garden maintenance of his own volition. Keeping busy and active would have eased boredom, frustration and irritability and the general distress it had caused the family. Gerald failed to turn the domestic environment into one of happiness and fulfilment. Unemployment decimated social relationships outside the house. He gave up golf, not only because of expense, but also because of the "embarrassment" of being unemployed. Voluntary work which substituted golf did not last long. Thus joblessness extinguished social contacts outside the family. What had once been a social-active lifestyle in employment had changed to a domestic-passive one in unemployment.

The moderately affected case:

The sadness of unemployment compared with the thought of the loss of life made Ross Timms realise how insignificant the benefits of employment were. The guilt of low family commitment in employment was redeemed after job loss with a "family first" philosophy, followed by other aspects of life. Unemployment with large blocks of unobligated time, enabled Ross to make positive changes and adjust his value system. He sustained himself by being useful at home, enjoying the garden and doing voluntary jobs. A marked change had occurred from an active-social to a domestic-active lifestyle.

The minimally affected case:

David's response to unemployment was a proactive one. He made choices about what he wanted to do, how, when and where he wanted to do it. He had the capabilities and competencies of assessing his personal and social world, predicting what the future might hold and making plans to deal with that future. Being inner-directed he was able to ascribe meaning to his personal and social worlds. Unemployment created opportunities for psychological fulfilment. It was characterised by choosing to initiate activities like piano-playing and working on the computer, when things were not going to plan, like the discontinuation of job search. He also re-perceived situations, like engaging in activities to enjoy himself in a relaxed and easy manner. These were valued directions which David chose in the absence of a regular job. He preserved the identity of an independent-minded and inner-directed person and maintained an active-social lifestyle.

Conclusions

The question raised was: Does the degree of job loss affect an individual's capacity to draw on his or her leisure capital? It was shown quite clearly that severely affected Gerald Green was unable to structure unobligated free time and was too depressed to engage in the other categories of experience using personal agency although he had competent handyman skills and excellent leadlighting abilities to sustain an absorbing hobby. These findings were consistent with the three cases of severely affected persons in the major sample of ten cases. Ross Timms, moderately affected showed positive adaptation after the initial adverse impact had worn off. Surviving the illness had a big effect. Importantly, he was able to change his value system from work- to family-orientated activity. Four cases were identified in the sample of ten in the major study and similar patterns of positive adaptation were observed. Family role re-negotiation was entered into willingly and proactivity in leisure activities during employment extended into unemployment albeit, after a short period of identity strain after job loss. David Patton saw unemployment as an opportunity for self-development and his engagement into serious leisure — piano-playing, computer and sporting activities — did much to sustain psychological well-being. Three of the ten cases in the major study were minimally affected, had excellent skills nurtured in non-occupational roles, and were able to sustain themselves with levels of high personal satisfaction. They were able to draw on their leisure capital to the extent that activities captivated and absorbed their attention. It can be concluded from the case studies examined in this paper that the degree of job loss impact does affect an individual's capacity to draw on his or her leisure capital. The level of activity participation tends to be proportional to the intensity of that impact. It is suggested that providers using leisure programmes to ameliorate the deprivations of unemployment take the impact of job loss into account when participants are accepted into schemes for the unemployed.

References

Bourdieu, P. (1985) *Distinction: A social critique of the judgement of taste.* London: Routledge and Kegan Paul.

Evans, S.T. and Haworth, J.T. (1991) 'Variations in personal activity, access to categories of experience and psychological well-being in unemployed young adults', *Leisure Studies*, Vol. 10, pp. 249-64.

Fryer, D. (1995a) Social and psychological consequences of unemployment: From interviewing to intervening?', in R. Hicks, P. Creed, W. Patton, and J. Tomlinson (eds) *Unemployment developments and transitions.* Brisbane: *Australian Academic Press*, pp. 58-76.

——— (1995b) 'Benefit agency? Labour market disadvantage, deprivation and mental health', *The Psychologist*, pp. 265-272.

Fryer, D.M. and Payne, R. (1984) 'Proactive behaviour in unemployment: findings and implications', *Leisure Studies*, Vol. 3: pp. 273-95.

—— (1986) 'Being unemployed: A review of the literature on the psychological experience of unemployment', in C. L. Cooper and I. Robertson (eds) *International review of industrial and organisational psychology*. Chichester: Wiley, pp. 235-278.

Glyptis, S. (1994) 'Leisure provision for the unemployed: imperative or irrelevant?', *World Leisure and Recreation*, Vol. 36, No. 4: pp. 34-39.

Haworth, J.T. (1997) *Work, leisure and well-being*. London: Routledge.

Haworth, J.T. and Ducker, J. (1991) 'Psychological well-being and access to categories of experience in unemployed young adults', *Leisure Studies*, Vol. 10: pp. 265-74.

Jahoda, M. (1979) 'The impact of unemployment in the 1930s and 1970s', *Bulletin of the British Psychological Society*, No. 32, pp. 309-314.

—— (1984) 'Social institutions and human needs: A comment on Fryer and Payne', *Leisure Studies*,Vol. 3: pp. 297-299.

—— (1986) 'In defence of non-reductionist social psychology', *Social Behaviour*, No. 1: pp. 25-29.

—— (1992) Reflections on Marienthal and after, Journal of Occupational and Organisational Psychology, 65, 355-358.

Kay, T. (1994) 'When great expectations reach their journeys end: accepting the limits of leisure provision of the unemployed', *World Leisure and Recreation*, Vol. 36, No. 4: pp. 29-33.

Lobo, F. (1996a) 'Coping with bulk unobligated time: The case of unemployment', *Loisir et Société*, Vol. 19, No. 2: pp. 377-413.

Lobo, F. (1996b) 'The effects of late career unemployment on lifestyle', *Loisir et Société*, Vol. 19, No. 1: pp. 167-194.

Stebbins, R.A. (1992) *Amateurs, professionals and serious leisure*. Montreal: McGill-Queen's University Press.

Stebbins, R.A. (1996) Serious leisure in the jobless future, Paper presented at the conference on "New Strategies for Everyday Life: Work, Free Time, and Consumption," Tilburg, The Netherlands, December.

Right or Commodity ?

Survival of Industry and the Countryside, and 'Green' Leisure Development in Post 'Resort Act 1987' Japan

Yohji Iwamoto

University of Reading

Introduction

Japan is not a singular or mysterious country. Although there used to be a kind of discourse, mainly by capitalists during the 1970s and 1980s, exaggerating Japan's uniqueness and praising its economic success as a miracle, we are realising now that it was a myth or a transitional phase of the development of domestic capitalism. Most of the advantageous characteristics of Japanese companies, including the open-ended employment system, are declining. On the other hand, the behaviour of the government seems to be unchanged. Its first priority since the Second World War has been to back up the business sector. It works in an almost socialistic manner in co-ordinating the business sector to prevent the loss of free competition. Such an attitude has been mirrored by most other Asian governments. Accordingly, Japanese leisure activities have shown characteristics of the 'other side of the coin' of domestic industrialism. Leisure has not been regarded as one of the human rights. Rather, Japanese leisure is a matter of economics as well as a matter of politics.

Leisure in Japan can be seen clearly if we view it in connection with the central policy of the country and the changing nature of inland capitalism. Such a methodology may also to some extent be appropriate to the examination of leisure activities in other Asian capitalist countries which also have a highly centralised government.

A brief history of the Japanese national development scheme and leisure policy

The historical background of leisure policy in Japan dates from the late 19th century with the expectation of getting foreign cash from overseas tourists. This changed drastically as a result of the structural transformation of the post-war Japanese economy. *The First National Development Scheme* of October 1962 pointed out that there was a necessity to develop in both the rural and urban fringe areas to encourage leisure activity, and also a need to maintain local balance by means of both industrial and leisure develop-ment. *The New National Development Scheme* of May 1969 underlined the need "To fund facilities for day trips and short stay recreation by public investment". The *Blue Print for Re-organising the National Land (Nippon Rettou Kaizou Ron)*, written privately by Prime Minister Tanaka in 1972, also referred to large-scale recreational zone development.

During the period of the rise of Japanese industrialism, the Tourism Policy Council (TPC) reports were on several occasions orientated towards a leisure policy. The first TPC report was launched in November 1967 in a period when Japanese overseas tourism had increased drastically. Entitled *How to Encourage Foreign Visitors and Organise Their Reception in the Changing Circumstances of International Tourism*, the report stressed the encouragement of overseas visitors to Japan because of the need to keep the balance of the international currency.

In April 1969, the second TPC report, entitled *The Nature and Future Prospects for Tourism in the National Life*, underlined the desire of urban working people for regeneration through tourism. Also, tourism was identified as a custodian of the natural environment. In July 1970, this was followed by another report, *For the Desirable Development of Tourism*, to add practical proposals to the previous report.

In August 1973, the third report *International Tourism, its Role and Policy* abandoned the role of tourism as a foreign cash generator. Since then the Commission has stopped working because the Minister of Transport did not request further reports. This period of silence might imply that this was the heyday of Japanese industrialism.

According to the *Maekawa Report* in 1986 which emphasised the require-ment for a drastic expansion of the home market to change the characteristics of the national economy, the *Fourth National Development Scheme*, July 1987 and the *Resort Act* of 1987 were important signs of the approach of the post-industrial stage of Japanese development. The enactment motivated the business sector to investigate the potential of long-stay luxury resort facilities. 16.2% of the national land became designated as resort areas under the Act. There was furious stock inflation during this period. In 1995 I reported to the LSA's Eastbourne Conference (Iwamoto, 1995) that such a development style brought devastating environmental hazards to the Japanese country-side. There were three characteristics of the leisure policy at this stage:

- it had lost the flavour of social welfare policy for workers. The business sector was regarded as its main promoter. This was often enhanced by de-regulation and establishing "daisan-sector" (which means the third sector), which was a joint venture with public and business sectors for profit making;

- it was a short-stay, high-cost type tourism under the pressure of the long working day and substantial increases in wages. However, the new resort trend was to keep the costs high while attempting to prolong the period of stay. An article in "the Mainichi" (news paper) of the 4th August 1992 supports this connection. A week's holiday for parents and two children cost, on average, £280 in the UK, £320 in France and £1,960 pounds in Japan (£1 = 250 yen);

- resort development activity, as a large-scale, money-making operation, disfigured the environment and disrupted the local community. It was especially the case where the local government strongly promoted the development to break the community into two. There were many development projects crucially delayed or suspended. Then the government, although the Resort Act looked ahead ten years, re-considered its framework in a critical way (Administrative Inspection Bureau, Prime Minister's Office, 1994).

The changing nature of Japanese Tourism industry can be summarised thus:

1870s–1960s .... targeted the overseas tourist in pursuit of foreign cash

1970s–1980s .... as a social welfare policy for urban workers

late 1980s–early 1990s ..... as a tool for expanding the domestic market

late 1990s–21st century ... an era of green tourism?

Green Tourism promotion policies: why green tourism now?

The ministries and departments of the Japanese government have a conventional way of thinking that they should encourage business 'underneath their umbrella'. Reasons for the popularity of 'green tourism' promotion are revealed by examining issues of survival for both Japanese agriculture and the tourism sector.

It was a policy document entitled *A Recommendation for Green Tourism, take a relaxing holiday in the rural villages*, produced by the Agricultural Structure Improvement Bureau, Ministry of Agriculture in July 1992, that focused on the possibility of green tourism furthering the survival of agriculture under the approaching GATT Uruguay round agreement. This also stimulated the tourism sector which was suffering from 'hollowing' or flattening out brought about by the structural shift in the domestic manufacturing industry, and green tourism was also identified as a good tool or methodology for its survival.

Ministry of Agriculture, Fishery and Forestry[1]

The *Recommendation for Green Tourism*[2] in 1992 promoted the notion that rural villages should be opened to the outside world to enable the establishment of a new thriving co-relationship with urban areas:

It is a fact that we have a much stronger preference than ever before for the idea of "back to nature" which is reflected in the fact that many people are currently attaching greater weight to mental richness and affordability under the conditions of a maturing inland economy. Accordingly, both agriculture and rural villages are regarded as having a renewed attraction.'

The document also expounds the idea of a Japanese style green tourism:

Its basic aim is to bring about a well balanced nation-wide development by the mutual support and coexistence of rural villages and urban cities, and to construct a bridge between the making of beautiful and open villages and an enjoyment of new leisure and love of rural space, both of which the urban dweller [has come to expect and appreciate]. [As to the points of the MoA report, see note 2.]

The background of the document is, I suggest, that:

- Japanese agriculture, in which the peak age of the farming workers population is nearly 70, is now threatened with extinction (Nougyoh-hakusyo Annual Report for Agriculture 1996, p.17). The political agreement at the GATT Uruguay round renewed the difficult circumstances;
- the agriculture of the marginal and mountain areas[3] is suffering in conditions of great difficulty because of their lower productivity. However, agriculture on the plains, especially on the urban fringe areas, is also threatened by, for example, non-supportive higher land tax, which taxes agricultural land at the same rate as land for residential home sites, so that agricultural owners are inclined to give up farming and release the land for housing;
- culturally, the Japanese custom whereby urban nuclear families come back home in mid-August and the New Year and spend several days with parents and relatives, is going to disappear as the generations pass;
- politically, there is a 'hidden agenda' to the ruling style of the central government. A good Ministry or department should get as large as possible an annual budget to distribute to those under its area of responsibility. There is little criticism that this is not environmentally friendly and so on. For the same reason, we can hardly ever find the words 'sustainable development' amongst the official reports except those of the Environmental Agency. What I want to say is that creating a new trend is in itself a good reason for the survival of any Ministry.

According to a survey by the MoA in September 1992, developing rural tourism was expected by local authorities in the mid/mountain areas to prove a best possible method to create new job opportunities (Nougyoh-hakusyo, 1996: p.27). In 1993, the Ministry of Agriculture started "the Green Tourism Model Development Project', 'Have a Relaxing Holiday in a Rural Village' (named after the German project; "Urlaub auf dem Bauernhof"), and so on. They promoted the 'Infrastructure Development Promoting the Act for the

Development of Leisure Activity by Staying in Rural Villages' of 1995. Thus the ministry is regarded as the leading actor in the promotion of Japanese rural tourism.

National Land Agency

The National Land Agency's concern for green tourism began from a re-consideration of the Resort Act 1987. The General Resort Area Development Study Group Interim Report *For Resort Development in the Future*, February 1993, made the following points [direct translation]:

> Resorts for the nation, for the community, and for the new national land construction.
>
> 1. If a family is to enjoy a proper lifestyle, they should enjoy a week's holiday at least once a year. To enable this to be arranged.
>
> 2. Local authorities should build up 'quality check system of resort activity' with the agreement of the relevant people in the local area.
>
> 3. There is also a need to examine co-operation in the promotion for the green tourism using the landscape and culture of the rural villages, and a methodology for the coexistence of agriculture, forestry and fisheries.
>
> 4. To activate the de-populated rural villages in the mid/mountain areas, there is a need to arrange rural resorts to increase the exchange of population with the urban cities, and for the urban dweller to play a role as the 'second' home community.

The document proposed the following:

> 1. It is necessary to provide high quality resort facilities for families to stay long term at reasonable cost. For this, a re-arrangement of the family stay facilities including the existing ones is needed together with and the provision of good information.
>
> 2. To encourage the nation to take regular holidays, arrangement should be made including the spread of the holiday season, establishment of long stay tourism, off-season holidays, flex-'vacances' etc. for family stays.
>
> 3. t]To consider the introduction of family discount tickets and off-peak tickets which would discourage crowding at the peak times.

The document has the basic aim of reviewing the resort boom which has been overheated by the 1987 Act and has been a highly expensive style of holiday for several reasons.

This report did not intend only to assist green tourism development, however. It is also remarkable that the previous flavour of some aspect of social welfare policy has returned as well as an attempt to properly appreciate leisure activities as part of national life. The first item implies, as in the previous MoA document, that the socio-cultural habits are going to be taken over by commercial activity. Another document also referred to this, saying "it is expected to be a growing market" (National Land Report 1996: p.62)

The National Land Agency anticipates structural changes in the inland economy in another part of the report, but there seems to be no comment about possible links between this and the role of leisure and tourism.

Ministry for Transport

The tourism sector, which is under the protection of the Ministry of Transport, is also put in a difficult situation. Here is the background information:

1. **Figure 1** shows the results of annual public opinion polls conducted by the Prime Minister's Office. To the question "which aspect of life do you give priority for the future?", for the first time in 1983 the responders rated their first priority as "leisure activities". By 1995, over one third of the responders prioritised this item.

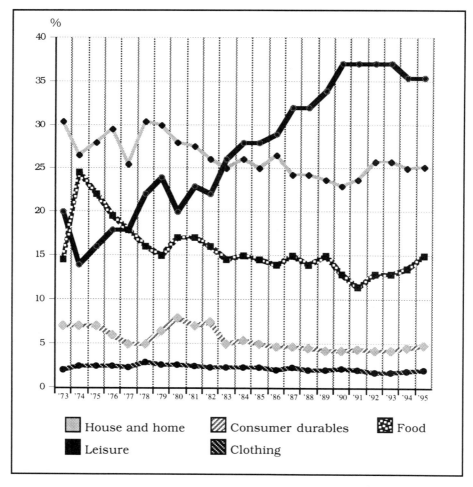

Figure 1 "Way of life' priority responses, 1973–1995

2. However, domestic tourism is in a disadvantageous position compared with tourism overseas. Japanese tourists to foreign countries reached over 15 million a year by 1995 (**Figure 2**). This represents a record-making 12.7% increase over the previous year. According to the higher yen rate (**Figure 3**), the main reason for choosing to travel abroad was that "it was relatively cheaper than travelling at home". 57.2% said this in June 1994 (Annual Report of Tourism: p.69).

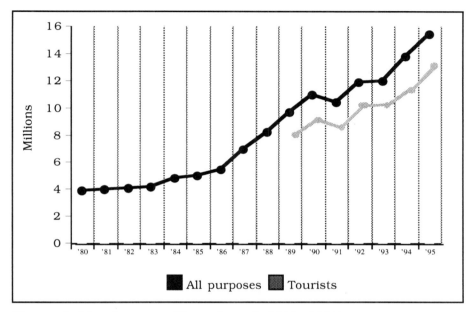

Figure 2   Number travelling abroad, 1980–1995

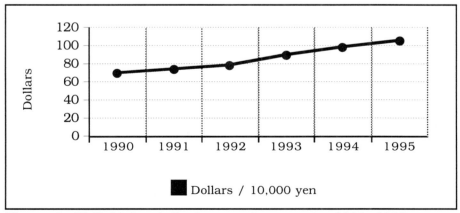

Figure 3   Shift in the dollar/yen exchange rate, 1990–1995

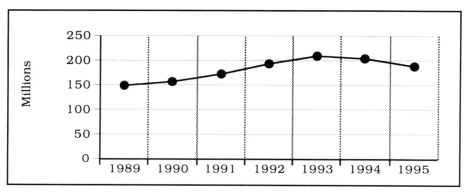

**Figure 4 Number of domestic tourists (not including day trips)
1989–1995**

3. On the other hand, the number of domestic tourists in 1995 declined
    by 8.0% compared to the previous year (**Figure 4**). Over half of the
    inland Hotels and Inns are in the red (ART, p. 73).

4. The smaller Japanese style inns ('ryokan'), many of which were con-
    structed during the 1960s and 1970s for recreational company trips,
    are facing difficulties in attracting new customers. The facilities are
    becoming old-fashioned. Most of them feel that the facilities are not fit
    for the fashionable single, small group and family tourists.

5. In addition to the facility problem, the ryokan are also facing difficulties
    in finding the successor of the small family business with over loaded
    work and unclear future prospects. The number of ryokan has
    decreased from 74,889 to 72,325 in the years 1991 to 1994 (ART: p.
    211).

It seems to me that the publication of the Tourism Policy Council report in
1995, after 22 blank years since the launch of the previous one, implies their
sense of crisis and that on the whole, its content strongly reflects the recent
socio-economic change in the country[4].

There is no reference to 'green tourism' in this document, but we can
understand that their stance is exactly the same as the previous two
Ministries when we see the following wording [proposal II-9, quoted from their
English version]:

> ... also it is an effective means of increasing people to people exchange
> and thus revitalising the areas that people concerned discover tourist
> attractions enabling visitors to feel the nature and local culture of
> farming and fishing villages and of forests and mountains areas with
> abundant natural assets, and that they develop tourist destinations
> featuring morning markets on their own.

Since the launch of the report, the Ministry of Transport has promoted the
policy according to the recommendations. The *Annual Report of Tourism 96*

stated:

> As for the inland tourism system, it mainly targets group visitors, in the so called "overnight stay with party dinner and breakfast style" and does not yet follow up the needs of the increasing numbers of individual, family and small group customers. Accordingly, inland tourism is facing a hollowing-out of the industry. It is necessary to change the inland travelling system drastically. On the other hand, sight-seeing development in the whole areas has the effect of activating the local culture and economy. It is expected to play an important part for the local development of the agricultural, forestry and fishery villages and the mid/mountain area etc. (ART 1996: p. 78)

The president of the Japanese Tourism Association also stated that "Tourism is an essential element for regional development" (*Tourism Strategy in the New Age* 1994, Preface).

Summary of the policy

Table 1 shows measures relating to green tourism development in the year

Table 1   Green tourism development, 1996

Title of measures	Office	Project	Annual budget
"Refresh Home Village" Model Case Promotion	National Land Agency	current 78 places, new 8 places	£4,320,850
Accommodation Arrangements in the De-Populated Areas	National Land Agency	current 10 places, new 10 places	£4,320,850
General Arrangements for the Exchanges Between Mountain Villages and Urban Cities	National Land Agency	current 2 places, new 3 places	£1,273,390
Nature Recreation Villages	Ministry of Agri-culture	current 379 places, development continuing 75 places, new 27 places	£37,336,830
'Holidays in the Mountain Villages'	Forestry Agency, MoA	development continuing 19 places, new 9 places.	£19,526,350
'Relaxing Holidays in the Rural Villages'	Ministry of Agri-culture		£1,620,700

of 1996 (source: *Annual Report of Tourism,* July 1996) as follows:

Recreation zones and facilities in the rural areas

(1) *Exchanges between the cities and rural villages.* There are also other measures by the MoA including 'Green Home Village FUREAI Project', 'Second Home Villages in the De-Populated Areas', 'Refresh Home Village', and 'Home Village C&C Model'.

(2) *Green tourism.* Based on the 'Act for Infrastructure Arrangements to Encourage the Staying Leisure Activities in the Rural Villages' of 1995, the following projects were provided: Farm Inn Management Guidance; training; publicity; promotion for the prefectures offices; promoting activities to encourage local plans.

The number of registered Accommodations by this Act is 422 bodies (Feb. 1996). The Environment Agency also has a register system for accommodations called 'Nature Inns' to encourage visitors to villages to enjoy nature watching.

Research activities

Since the launch of the MoA report in 1992, the academic community (including geographers, town and rural planners as well as those with a background in agricultural subjects) has been showing an interest in green tourism. This trend may reflect the availability of research budgets from the government. There are some common themes as follows:

1. The academics are usually critical about the previous resort boom. Most of the discussions tried to link the green tourism issue with a broader socio-economic context as follows (Sakai. K, pp. 20-31, Nihon Kanko Kyokai, ed, 1995):

    * the increase in wages and consumption.
    * the increase in free and leisure time.
    * the shift towards an ageing society.
    * the increase in the numbers of working women and fewer babies.
    * the diffusion of 'life-long education'.
    * internationalisation.
    * global environmental issues.
    * the advance of telecommunications technology

    They appreciate the diversified aspects of green tourism. However, some of them are worried that the policy could tend to lead to a narrower and more specific perception of green tourism because of the policies' incentive effect. For example, there is such criticism for the current policies especially in the specific project level that:

    * they tend to restrict the green tourism solely to a narrow matter of farm

inn development rather to the total promotion.

• the principle that the local people should have the first priority may not be appreciated properly. The support system for the individual farmer's family is still unclear.

• practically, the legal framework for the provision of accommodation is too strict for the farmers because this intends to control the professional hotel providers. (Yamazaki, M. Inoue et 1996, p.142)

2. The study of European models, mainly from UK, France, Germany, and Italy, is one of the main interests of the researchers, and aims to encourage Japanese farmers to take action. Such foreign information includes not only the interview with the farm inns hosts but also the legal framework and support system of the respective country. The lack of American influence is very unusual in the post-war history of Japan.

3. They are trying to encourage the creation of a Japanese-style green tourism because they realise such European cases are not applicable to Japan because of the differences of the socio-cultural background. They are also compiling information from the pioneering cases in Japan.

There are several problems for Japanese green tourism.

• *Facility:*   It is difficult to provide accommodation in the same building that the host family lives in because of the privacy problem. Historically, agrarian reforms after the Second World War dismantled farming estates in order to re-distribute the arable land to the former field workers. This led in the rural areas to a lack of buildings suitable for conversion to guest houses.

• *Time:*   Japanese agriculture is still highly labour intensive, and is carried on by an ageing community. They cannot spare time to have guests especially during the busy summer time, which overlaps with the tourism season. The lack of a B&B system in the country is also one of the obstacles and is regarded as a problem to be sorted out in the future.

• *Provider:*   It is reported that some of the farm inns were opened not by the local people, but by the newcomers who could afford to meet the initial investment for new purpose-built accommodation,

• *Legal obstacles:*   Other problems in starting such businesses have been reported. The legal regulations and procedures are regarded as too complicated and too strict for 'second business' people. The stubborn current legal system does not allow 'second business' people to make less rigid arrangements.

• *Additional attraction and 'life-long learning':* Some of the pioneering farm inns in Hokkaido are offering special programmes including sheep-shearing, weaving, herb, craft and jam-making sessions and so on to give additional value. Most of them look rather Western, definitely not on the lines of Japanese rural culture. They are said to be trying to meet the needs of the city people. It may not make the foreign visitors very happy. Such attractions are sometimes called 'life long learning', departing from the original UNESCO concept of adult education.

• **Lack of amenity in the countryside**: Most of the Japanese rural villages do not have enough facilities such as museums to show the hospitality or unspoilt landscape which would attract visitors. This is a task of the community for the future. It may be a basic dilemma that the Ministries, with much stronger centralised governing power than any of the local authorities, are promoting the notion of local characteristics by local people.

• **The negative image of the countryside**: In the Japanese language, "countryside chap" has long been a childish insult like "stupid". Historically, the rural areas have been regarded as a place of production for urban people and scarcely been regarded as even a place to enjoy living in. These areas have suffered from poverty for a long time, and are disadvantaged compared to urban life even now. The memory of previous poverty is not easily overcome and it is difficult to convert to the notion of countryside as a place of hospitality. In addition to this, there is a conventional and complicated human relationship which demands both financial and physical obligations to support local community.

• **Lack of the national voice to promote the value of countryside**: In Japan, there has been no romantic poet like Wordsworth who praised the value of the countryside, no talented storyteller like Beatrix Potter who created lovely animal characters, no national movement like the early Council for the Preservation of Rural England to protect the threatened rural landscape.

All of these are tasks for the future.

Some examples

The actual spread of the new green tourism movement from top to bottom is rather slow. Some of the earliest examples include:

JA: In the private sector, JA (Japanese Agriculture Union) launched an important policy document in 1991 entitled *Comfortable My Village and My Town Development,* based on *Agriculture for the 21st Century, Rural Village Development* and JA's Policy. In this document, amongst the seven policies were 'Organising farm inn department by levelling-up of services and facilities, the construction of garden cities and rural resort arrangements'. They targeted the development of visitor reception such as farm inns, agriculture parks, allotments, second homes, children's villages and so on. The large-scale resort development boom was still influential at that time. It is unclear how these policies were effective or whether the JA people appreciated to any extent the notion of green tourism.

Co-ops: The oldest and biggest Japanese co-operative, Co-op Kobe opened 'the Co-op Home Village, Chickusa' for its members in 1994 (Inoue 1996.

pp. 62-67). Many of the urban consumers' co-ops have arranged contracts with the farmers for direct purchase in quest of safer crops produced by less chemical, more organic methods. This has the potential to enable some sort of green tourism to flourish using existing human contacts. However the facilities may not be open to the public.

Private farm inns in Hokkaido: Several farm inns have opened in Hokkaido, Japan's most northern and the second biggest island. Its land-

Table 2   Examples of farm inn accommodation, 1995

Category of farming	Provision	Accommodation fee (£1 = 200 yen)	Capacity
sheep farmstead 40/9ha (newly started two years ago)	farm inn & restaurant	£32.5 (weekday) £37.5 (weekend) with supper and breakfast.	4 bedrooms (considering future extension)
stud horse farmstead	restaurant, craft shop & farm inn	self catering cottages £140 for 10 persons, £75 for 5 (per night)	two cottages
organic vegetable and herb farmstead	farm inn & restaurant, as well as direct retail service	£15 with supper and breakfast	n/a
rice and vegetable farmstead (10ha in total)	PYO(0.7a) and direct retail service.	fees reported as cheap 'Youth Hostel' style inn	n/a
rice and vegetable farmstead (130a)	allotment (1ha, 100m^2 per section)	4 family rooms (under construction)	n/a

scape is similar to that of Europe and its farmsteads are the biggest in Japan. There were farm inn seminar groups in five towns. The prefecture office was reported as supporting them. Here are several examples (see **Table 2**).

There were 14 farm inns in Hokkaido in July 1995; 5 offered self-catering, the rest provided two meals (Yamazaki 1996, p. 160). There are few B&Bs. How the local community should show hospitality to visitors and still make a profit from them, and how to activate the whole local community, is the task for the future.

Discussion

Current Japanese discussion of green tourism seems devoid of any clear appreciation of the positive notion of 'green' which differentiates this from merely rural tourism. It is noteworthy that Japanese green tourism policy has a flavour of social welfare for the nation. However, the basic tone is one of survival strategy for the declining mid mountain areas, agriculture and the tourism industry. In my view, local initiatives and empowerment for them seem essential to enable attractive local development. The conventional method of the government — designation and funding of pilot cases for local authority officers to examine and copy in their own districts — should be re-considered.

The government seems to take the view that national demand for leisure will everlastingly increase. The often-cited results of annual public opinion polls, "Preferences of the nation for the way of life in the future" (see Figure 1), are used to justify the needs for future leisure development without consideration of the wider picture. The failure of the previous resort boom should be seen as evidence.

Another reason for this is the declining desire for "house and living". Many working people in the metropolitan areas faced astronomical increases in land and housing prices, and had to give up their dreams of home owner-ship. One effect of this during the late 1980s in Japan was that retail sales of the top-of-the-line model Toyota "Crown" outstripped sales of the cheaper previous best-seller model "Corolla", as disappointed potential home-buyers invested instead in the best possible luxury car.

As in the previous large-scale resort development boom, which has also been declining since the end of the boom in 1993, it seems that the dis-cussion has been based on the supplier side. It would be reasonable to consider the issue from the customer side.

Following is an analysis of the household economy of a young couple without children, reported in the April 1997 issue of a monthly magazine for housewives (Nikkei-Shopping, April 1997). The couple in question had asked for specialist advice about the economic implications of their wish to have a car and three children.

Monthly Living Costs of a Young Japanese Household: (£1=200YEN)

Income	£	£	£
husband (29 years old, FT officer worker)	1,712.50		
wife (28 years old, PT office worker)	1,000.00		
income sub-total			2,712.50
Expenditure			
mortgage (inc. maintenance)		−698.00	
insurance+pension		−200.00	
gas/water/electricity		−187.50	
pocket money (for two)		−350.00	
miscellaneous		−303.00	
food & drink		−290.00	
leisure*		−283.30	
clothing		−100.00	

social expenses	−100.00
deposit account	−100.00
expenditure sub-total	−2,611.80
Current balance:	100.70

The couple were advised to fundamentally re-organise their family planning: give up the car and one of the possible babies, as well as cut down on extra expenditure including half of their leisure expenses. "Otherwise", they were advised, "you will be £100,000 in the red in by 2005, £200,000 by 2014 and £300,000 by 2020".

Most Japanese families have to survive under the lowest ever interest rate (currently 0.25%) and increased consumer's tax (from 3% to 5% on the 1st April, 1997). There is also a campaign warning that banks could go bankrupt in the future to achieve a Japanese Big Bang (de-regulation and reformation of financial system).

In addition, the hollowing out of the domestic industry is becoming rather rapid. The government reports definitely that "Leading industries like steel, electronic appliances, car manufacturing and so on which were the main force of the post-war Japanese economy have been declining" (NLA 96, p. 46).

The Ministry of International Trade and Industry forecast that 8.4% of the manufacturing sector would shift abroad in 1994, and 10% in 1995. This does not necessarily mean the transfer of the older technology. Their questionnaire to the Japanese manufacturing companies which had factories in

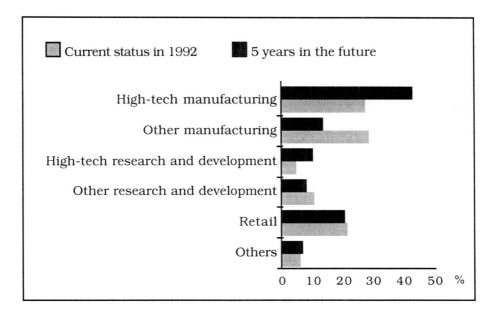

**Figure 5   Shift of industry to Asian countries and
           its change in quality**

Asia in 1994 revealed that 28% of them were already using production methods which required the same as or more advanced technology than their Japanese factories, and that the figure would increase to 42% in five years (NLA96, p.29) (see **Figure 5**).

The government uses unclear wording to describe such a situation:

> The decrease in the number of employment opportunities, and new developments in the service sector are expected to create reasonable job prospects.

Official reports never mention that such a hollowing out is likely to bring mass unemployment in the near future nor is there any attempt to try to halt or at least to discourage the shift of industry abroad.

The unemployment rate in Japan is currently at its worst-ever level but could increase further. It can easily be seen that Japanese society is now entering a completely new stage. For example, the so called "low price strategy" was welcomed by most people when it was introduced for specific imported consumer goods several years ago. This was going to be expanded over many aspects of national life. Some of us realise that it has turned out to be merely an enhanced exploitation of the worker. The government should adjust the re-distribution system properly if it does not want to jeopardise the national lifestyle.

On the other hand, actual working hours have been increasing, contrary to the official statistics. The difference has been firstly brought by, ironically, legal effort in the late 1980s to compress working hours in response to the US pressure during the "trading conflict", and the adoption of "*syu-kyuu hutuka sei*" which means "two days off a week system". This led to the increase of illegal and unpaid extra work on weekdays. The re-structuring policy, which merely means cutting of personnel expenses since the burst of the "bubble economy", made the situation worse. It is not an exaggeration that the white-collar workers go home by the last commuter train from offices in central Tokyo to sleep four or five hours and return to the office in the morning. Commuting itself may take three hours. The elite officers of the government are no exception. One at the Ministry of Justice confessed privately the unexpected deaths from overwork and suicide amongst colleagues, adding that her department was not the worst. It is difficult to measure such a hidden aspect properly — however this is the reality.

The success of green tourism may have the potential to play an important part not only in the conservation of the national land but also in assuring the quality of national life. It seems to me that this requires special supportive action in other ways, including, for example, the signing up of the government for the ILO treaty No.132 as well as the promotion of the notion of work-sharing in the country to maximise limited job opportunities as a matter of social justice. In other words, the dilemma is how should people still defend the right to enjoy leisure in the countryside under the condition that the countryside has been increasingly converted into a commodity under a market mechanism.

Notes

1   Hereafter, simply 'Ministry of Agriculture.
2   The points of the "Recommendation for Green Tourism" are as follows:

> *"1,   National life in the future and green tourism.*
>
> • *There is an increasing appreciation of the multi-functional aspects of the rural (agricultural, mountain and fishery) villages and the relaxed life which is possible there. As a reflection of the changing values of the nation which prefers mental to material richness. On the other hand, there is an urgency to activate the rural areas so as to continue a well-balanced national land development because the areas have become less and less animated.*
>
> • *For this purpose, as well as promoting agriculture, forestry and fishery, it is important to energise the countryside areas and to create beautiful rural spaces by identifying the areas as "living spaces" and "leisure spaces".*
>
> • *From this viewpoint, it is important to recognise the promotion of green tourism as a crucial policy to activate the rural areas and to construct a co-existence relationship between urban cities and rural villages, and to advocate this over a longer time span.*
>
> *2,   Advocating green tourism.*
>
> • *Green tourism is recommended as "a long stay leisure activity to enjoy the natural environment, local culture, and human relationships in the green rural areas". In other words, the aim should be to encourage "an enjoyable relaxing holiday in the rural villages", as a bridge between the desire to create beautiful villages in the rural areas and the dream of urban dwellers to enjoy a new style of leisure activity and relaxation in those areas.*
>
> • *Green tourism has to maximise the use of local resources without large-scale development, to have high regard for human interchange including mental contact, and to contribute to the natural environment and the local community in the countryside. It is also important that the rural village side should take the initiative in general agreement, and regard this as a method of village development, and to promote it, aiming at "a rural village where both the resident and community are well activated".*
>
> • *Green tourism should bring economic advantage to the rural village, thus enabling it to continue. There should also be other advantages, that is to say, enhancing local pride and understanding of local industry, the accumu-lation of everyday life related and culture related stock. Encouragement of the younger generation to leave urban cities to return to the home town for new job opportunites.*
>
> • *For the urban dweller, on the other hand, the rural village is not just a pastime but a place for self-fulfilment, by enjoying and appreciating rural life and culture and by deepening understanding, by realising the relation-ship with natural environment, and re-creation of human nature.*

> • The areas where green tourism will be enjoyed should be areas where several conditions apply, that is, where agriculture, forestry and fishery production are working and can be seen and actively enjoyed, where there are excellent natural conditions, including vegetation, water and landscape, and where there is a rich cultural tradition and local support for the green tourism.

3,   The promotion of green tourism.

3.1 promotion of beautiful village-making.

Integrated infrastructure arrangements for both local productivity and living should be produced.

Consideration of the framework for the protection of the local landscape is needed. Also agreements and regulations etc. should be reached.

3.2 Arrangements for the urban dweller reception system.

Improvement of the service level. Personnel training for instructors. Arrangements for accommodations, etc.

Consideration of the registration system etc. for accommodation.

3.3 The promotion of systematic co-operation for PR activities and the construction of a feedback system of the requirements of the urban city side.

3.4 Arrangements for the promotion and support system.

Consideration of an active campaign on both urban and rural sides with the close co-operation of government and the local sector.

Consideration of systematic arrangements by the business sector, consumers' associations, trade unions, urban agricultural co-ops etc. to encourage visitors to the rural villages.

Consideration of a controlling system for the promotion of green tourism (state, prefectures, and cities, towns and villages offices) and co-operative relationships and divisions of role.' (RGT, MoA 1992)

3   There are four categories of land in Japan.
   i.   Urban areas = populated 500/km2.
   ii. Flat agriculture areas = those where flat arable land occupies over 20% of the areas.
   iii. Mid agricultural areas = covered with 50-80% of forest, with sloping arable land.
   iv. Mountain agricultural areas = covered with over 80% of forest, less than 10% arable land.
Categories iii. and iv. are usually called 'mid-mountain', which contains 62% of local authorities (2,014); 27% of population (33,000,000); 78% of national land (291,000 km2). It is regarded as playing an important role in: Production of agriculture, forestry and fisheries; Environment, and land conservation; Provision of living and leisure space; Preserving traditional, local culture. Its problems are: De-population and ageing: Not suitable for business; Decrease of local activities; Decrease of conservation facilities; To maintain the local communities in the areas is becoming

difficult: "it is increasingly difficult to invite manufacturing industry to such areas as used to be the case because of the higher Yen and the structural changes in the economy and industry" (National Land Report 1996, National Land Agency. p.55).

4   *General Direction in which Japan's Future Tourism Policies Should Be Set.* Proposed by the Tourism Policy Council (quoted from their English text.)

June 2, 1995

> *I. BASIC VIEWPOINTS ON TOURISM*
>
> 1.   *Everybody has the right to travel.*
>
> 2.   *Japan should strive to become a nation based on leisure tourism activities, not just a nation based on manufacturing.*
>
> 3.   *The tourism industry is a key industry which can lead the Japanese economy in the 21st century and create new employment opportunities.*
> 4.   *Large-scale reforms should be carried out in the domestic travel system.*
> 5.   *Tourism enables people to discover and create culture and develops areas.*
> 6.   *International tourism will promote mutual understanding between Japan and the rest of the world and correct Japan's trade imbalance.*
> 7.   *Tourism should be the good protector of a cultural heritage, natural environment and local traditions.*
>
> II   *PROPOSAL FOR CONCRETE MEASURES TO CREATE TOURISM IN THE 21ST CENTURY*
> 1.   *The "leisurely vacation" should be realized so that people in all walks of life can travel.*
> 2.   *Disabled and aged peoples should be encouraged to travel more, and an environmental facilitation travel for them should be established.*
> 3.   *Comprehensive effort should be made to improve the quality of tourism services and promotion of the tourism industry.*
> 4.   *Higher educational institutions such as a tourism University should be established to train personnel for employment in the travel industry.*
> 5.   *High-grade systems to provide information on tourism services, and useful tourism statistics should be available.*
> 6.   *Domestic travel arrangements should be changed by introducing lower prices and diversifying systems of prices and services.*
> 7.   *Facilities for travellers who stay in a destination for an extended time or travel around with a base in one places should be improved, and systems to facilitate such travel developed.*
> 8.   *A tourist destination of their own should be created by those concerned in an area receiving tourists, taking the initiative to work out a regional tourism promotion plan in co-operation with the travel industry in areas that generate tourism.*
> 9.   *Tourist attractions incorporating elements unique to a particular area should be promoted.*

10. *International tourism exchange should be expanded through activities at bilateral tourism councils and international tourism contributions through tourism-related international organizations.*
11. *Systematic international co-operation should be given to countries with priority, based on a clearly defined assistance policy.*
12. *Foreign visitors to Japan should be increased by promoting international conventions, lowering travel prices, and facilitation travel in Japan.*
13. *Tourist destinations should be developed with preservation of the natural environment and culture taken into account.*

III HOW POLICIES SHOULD BE IMPLEMENTED
1. *Formation of Basic Policy and Action Programs*
2. *Establishment of Goals*

Implementation of Action Programs (source, Kanko gyosei kenkyukai 1995, pp. 173-193).

References

Iwamoto, Y. (1995) 'The price of progress: Trends in leisure development in Japan', in G. McFee, W. Murphy, and G. Whannel (eds) *Leisure cultures: Values, Genders, Lifestyles* (LSA Publication No 54). Eastbourne: Leisure Studies Association, pp. 263-272.

The following books are in Japanese:

Administrative Inspection Bureau, Management and Co-ordination Agency, Prime Minister's Office., (1994) *Resort kousouno tyakujituna jitugen ni mukete (Toward a steady development of resort projects)* Tokyo: Administrative Inspection Bureau. ISBN

Inoue, K. Nakamura, O. and Yamazaki, M.. (1996-3) Nihongata green tourism (Japanese style green tourism). Tokyo: Toshibunkasya. ISBN 4-88714-170-X.

Kaneko, G. (1996-8) *Den-en resort no jidai (An age of rural resort)*. Tokyo: Shimizu-Kobundo. ISBN 4-87950-529-3.

Kankogyosei Kenkyukai (Research group for tourism policy) (1995-8) *Kanko rikkokuheno senryaku (A strategy for a state based on tourism with an explanation of "General Direction in which Japan's Future Tourism Policies Should Be Set" by the Tourism Policy Council)*. Tokyo: Nihon Kanko Kyokai. ISBN 4-88894-055-X.

Management and Co-ordination Agency, Prime Minister's Office (1996-11) *Koureikasyakai hakusyo (Annual report for an ageing society)*. Tokyo: Printing Bureau, Ministry of Finance. ISBN 4-17-190071-9.

Nourin Toukei Kyoukai (Institute for Agricultural Statistics) (1996-5). Tokyo: Nourin Toukei Kyoukai. ISBN 4-541-02097-1.

National Land Agency (1996-7) *Kokudo report (National land report)*. Tokyo: Printing Bureau, Ministry of Finance. ISBN 4-17-190810-8.

Nihon Kanko Kyokai (Japan Tourism Association). (1995-10) *Sinjidai no kanko senryaku vol. 1/2 (A tourism strategy of new age)*. Tokyo: Nihon Kanko Kyokai. ISBN 4-88894-029-0 / 4-88894-030-4.

Nihon Kanko Kyokai (Japan Tourism Association) (1996-7) *Sisatu koutekiti guide (A guidebook for advanced cases for inspection)*. Tokyo: Nihon Kanko Kyokai. ISBN 4-88894-045-2.

Planning and Co-ordination Bureau, National Land Agency, Prime Minister's Office. (1987) *Daiyonji zenkoku sougoukaihatu keikaku (The fourth national development scheme)*. Tokyo: Printing Bureau, Ministry of Finance. ISBN 4-17-250901-0.

Prime Minister's Office. (1996-7) *Kanko hakusyo (Annual report of tourism)*. Tokyo: Printing Bureau, Ministry of Finance. ISBN 4-17-155171-4.

Research Bureau, Economic Planning Agency, Prime Minister's Office (1996-12) *Nihonkeizai no genkyo (Current status of Japanese economy)*. Tokyo: Printing Bureau, Ministry of Finance. ISBN 4-17-310772-2.

Wakita, T. and Ishihara, T. (eds) (1996-4) *Kanko kaihatuto tiikisinko (Tourism development and regional development — green tourism, explanation and cases)*. Tokyo: Kokonsyoin. ISBN 4-7722-1659-6.

Yamazaki, M., Oyama, Y. and Ohshima, J. (1993-5) *Green Tourism*. Tokyo: Iyenohikari Kyokai. ISBN 4-259-54428-4.

IV

Leisure and City-Centre Regeneration

Leisure Property as an Indicator of the Changing Vitality and Viability of Town Centres: A Case Study

Martha Rowley
University of Reading

Neil Ravenscroft
University of Surrey

Introduction

Although many towns' retail centres have flourished over the last few years, there is a growing recognition that this pattern of growth has not been uniform. In particular, while remaining generally popular for comparison shopping (clothing, shoes, books and electrical goods, for example), town centres have become less attractive for other uses, notably DIY and some types of leisure attraction, particularly cinemas, bowling alleys, ice skating rinks and bingo halls.

While property specialists St Quintin (1997) argue that the relocation of the leisure uses has been associated with increasing traffic congestion, limitations on car parking and a growing fear of crime, the Urban and Economic Development Group (URBED), in its report to the Department of the Environment (DOE) on 'vital and viable town centres' (URBED, 1994), suggests that the shifts are related to the broader, changing role of town centres. In particular, as both population and employment have dispersed from towns, their centres have increasingly lost their role as the hub of social life. Changing work and living patterns, associated with the growth of the 'self-service' economy, have thus created new time and space-related demands for retail and leisure consumption, increasingly concentrated on the development of specialist retail and leisure parks in edge-of-town locations with easy car access, adequate free above-ground car parking and private security (St Quintin, 1997; DTZ Debenham Thorpe, 1997). This trend has been exacerbated by the overwhelming predominance of private finance for new developments (Carroll, 1997), particularly as developers seek to secure institutional funding (St Quintin, 1997).

In responding to the implications of this situation, particularly in terms of its potential impact on policies associated with sustainable development, central government has become increasingly committed to the concept of the compact city (Fulford, 1995). In reflecting the proposals contained in the European Commission Green Paper on the Urban Environment (CEC, 1990), that all future development should be concentrated on the compact, functionally mixed city, recent UK government policies on the environment (DOE, 1990), sustainable development (DOE, 1994) and transport (DOE and Welsh Office, 1994) have supported this view. As a result, town centre land use planning guidance (DOE and Welsh Office, 1993) has increasingly sought to emphasise the continuing role of the town centre as an appropriate location for retail and leisure development, with local authorities called upon to promote mixed land uses and support the retention and development of leisure and cultural facilities.

This guidance has recently been enhanced further, with the 1996 revisions (DOE, 1996) underlining the significance of town centre management, principally in developing clear standards of service provision and promoting environmental improvements in town centres. In addition, however, the recent guidance also includes a provision for local authorities to become more directly involved in the development process, principally through the assembly and designation of suitable town centre sites, particularly for leisure, cultural and mixed use developments.

While promoting town centre management and the encouragement of non-retail and office development, however, the DOE and Welsh Office (1993) concedes that not only is it difficult to establish what part management plays in maintaining the quality and health of town centres, but it is also difficult to establish suitable measures of these attributes. In addressing this issue of measurement, URBED (1994) suggests that it revolves around attractions, accessibility, amenity and action:

> It is... important to look at the underlying components of a healthy town centre, and these can be analysed through a health check that considers the attractions in terms of diversity and critical mass, accessibility in terms of mobility and linkages, amenity in terms of security and identity, and action in terms of organisational capacity and resourcing. (URBED, 1994: p. 54)

Central to the new guidance on maintaining and enhancing town centres are the twin concepts of vitality and viability. The first measure refers to how busy a town centre is at different times and locations, while the second relates to the continuing ability of the town centre to attract investment. The two are therefore interrelated, with the relative level of 'busyness' (vitality) seen as a significant component in new investment decisions (viability) and, concurrently, the continued development of new facilities (viability) generating an enhanced attraction for visitors (vitality).

Leisure and cultural development, particularly related to 'after hours' or evening use of town centres, is viewed as an important means of generating a new urban vitality (Comedia, 1991 and Bach, 1997), reflecting Jacobs' (1961) long-standing arguments that successful cities are those which can sustain a diverse range of uses which attract significant numbers of people. While some of the 'traditional' town centre leisure attractions, such as cinemas and bowling alleys, may be decentralising therefore, they are being replaced by a much more diverse range of smaller, predominantly locally owned and operated enterprises. These are often related to the entertainment, food and beverage markets, but also encompass specialist retail, cultural, recreational and educational uses.

While not being of individual economic significance, it is increasingly widely advocated that these leisure-based activities are capable of contributing positively to the regeneration of town centres (Bach, 1997), in some cases generating up to 15 per cent of local Gross Domestic Product (Comedia, 1991), depending on their "... critical mass and... level of economic maturity" (Montgomery, 1995a, p. 103). This is based, Montgomery argues, on increasing the volume of transactions which can take place in town centres:

> Providing the space for transactions across the day and night is what cities have always done, in any culture at any point in time. It is what cities are good at.... In this sense, the notion of urban vitality and the related concept of the evening economy is really only about opening up the possibilities for transactions to take place in longer and more extended segments of time. (1995a: p. 106)

This, then, is the central tenet of the argument for the promotion of leisure and cultural development in sustaining the health of town centres: that in generating both new production and new consumption, these activities seek to restore and underpin the original rationality for the existence of urban areas. The paper thus addresses directly the nature, role and significance of leisure and cultural production and its related consumption, by considering the evolving nature of the town centre as market place, in terms of the identities and cultures of both traders and consumers. As a consequence, the paper also addresses the nature and identity of spaces and the public realm, particularly in considering the social and cultural outcome of the changing physical structure of town centres and the impact which this has on those using (or being excluded from) these spaces.

Property and the production of leisure attractions

The physical basis of leisure and cultural development is property, either rented or owned, to the extent at least that most facilities and attractions occupy discrete spaces in town centres. While leisure property is addressed in a number of property texts (see, for example, Ratcliffe, 1978, Stapleton, 1986, Britton, *et al.*, 1989 and Butters, 1992), as well as some related to leisure and recreation (see, for example, Ravenscroft, 1992 and Swarbrooke, 1995), the predominant explanation and categorisations rarely extend beyond listings. While these typologies sometimes refer to factors such as ownership or market-type, they are dominated by physical classifications derived from Clawson and Knetsch's (1966) constructs of the perceived degree of artificiality introduced to 'natural' sites and are, consequently, of little relevance to built, urban, leisure properties.

In seeking alternative ways of distinguishing or identifying leisure properties, Williamson (1994) applies legal principles, in recognising that such properties are a form, or category, of real property. Although not separately referred to in law, a number of distinct leisure uses of property are recognised within statutory planning law, in the Town and Country Planning (Use Classes) Order 1987. This Order identifies groups, or classes, of uses of property which have similar characteristics, so that permission to use the property for one purpose also includes the express right to use it for all the other purposes in the class, without recourse to a fresh planning application. The classes dealing explicitly with 'leisure property' are as follows:

Class A3   The sale of food and drink for consumption on the premises or off the premises in the case of hot food, covering wine bars, public houses, restaurants and cafes.

Class C1   Hotels and hostels which do not provide any significant element of care.

Class D2   Many indoor sporting and leisure uses, except those using firearms or involving motorsport. This class specifically refers to cinemas, concert halls, bingo halls, casinos, dance halls, swimming pools, skating rinks, gymnasia and indoor leisure centres.

It is the accumulation of these types of property, together with other cultural and sporting facilities such as galleries and stadia, which contribute to the growth and distinctiveness of leisure attractions within many towns. In commenting on the nature of these forms of leisure property, Williamson (1994) suggests that they have two principal features which distinguish them from other forms of property: that the value of the property arises from the value of the business, rather than being independent of it, as is the case with many other types of property; and that the business invariably involves inviting people onto the premises for the purposes of activity, entertainment or recreation. As a consequence of these factors, particularly the former, most leisure properties have either been owner-occupied or subject to localised private rental, with little interest shown from corporate investors.

As Montgomery (1995a) suggests, this remains very much the case with town centre properties, where small-scale flexibility and limited space requirements are significant. As a consequence, the market for these properties is seen by property agents to be both marginal and risky, compared to other sectors of the town centre property market, particularly those relating to prime retail and office buildings. Away from town centres, however, the situation is changing rapidly, with institutions showing increasing interest in investing in leisure property, particularly purpose-built, mixed leisure developments such as the new wave of leisure parks being built throughout Europe (Europroperty, 1997). Located in both suburban and edge-of-town locations, the investment yields expected on these properties are now comparable with those for good retail and office properties:

> The synergy between uses creates the value of the leisure park concept. Visitors to these schemes on average utilise two or more of the activities on each visit, food being the most common secondary attraction. (St. Quintin, 1997: p. 7)

At present, therefore, it would seem that there is an inverse relationship operating between leisure property yields and proximity to town centres, with the prime locations being edge-of-town and the poorer ones being in the centre of towns. This certainly questions the wisdom and long term sustainability of promoting the development of cultural quarters in town centres, as well as being contrary to government land use planning policy guidance (DOE, 1996). More fundamentally, it also suggests that the current growth of leisure businesses in town centres may not be as a result of the increasing economic strength and attraction of those areas and, thus, may not contribute as fully to towns' vitality and viability as some advocates suggest.

Reading Town Centre Pilot Study

In order to test this theorisation, together with its resultant implications, this section reports on the findings of an empirical study on the measurement and application of the concepts of vitality and viability, using a 10-year time series of data for Reading, from 1985-95. The study covered property occupation and values, pedestrian flows and public attitudes to and usage of the town centre, supplemented by evidence about leisure property in the greater Reading area (see Ravenscroft, *et al.*, 1997).

Thirteen areas within the town centre were selected for the compilation of location-specific data. These comprise individual streets which have been grouped according to common retail and property occupation characteristics and geographical location. They therefore represent distinct areas within the town centre. Location-specific information was collected for each property in each area, the results of which were indexed and combined in order to analyse the health of the town centre. Additional work has since been done to extend the analysis to leisure properties outside the town centre.

In contrast to the traditional boundaries of the primary retail area of the town centre (the area enclosed by Broad Street, Friar Street, West Street and Market Place) the results for 1995, the most recent study period, indicate that this is changing. Rather than the former ubiquitous concentration on retail premises, there is an increasing concentration of the primary shopping area in the south west of the centre (the west end of Broad Street and the Broad Street Mall), accompanied by a shift in the pattern of property occupation in the increasingly peripheral, secondary locations elsewhere in the centre. In particular, there is a noticeable influx of leisure-related occupiers in these areas, often associated with food and beverage sales (especially bars and restaurants).

The strongest examples of this, as indicated in **Figure 1**, are Friar Street, to the east of the prime retail area, and the St Mary's Butts/Gun Street area to the south west. Data derived from recent planning applications (Reading Borough Council, 1996) indicate the extent of this shift. In the period from the beginning of 1995 to March 1996, the single largest net change in floorspace in the town centre occurred with respect to the Class D2 planning category of assembly and leisure (+156,000 square metres) and the Class A3 planning category of food and beverages premises (+14,540 square metres). Combined, these represent 17.5% of the total net change in planning commitments over this period.

Recent surveys about people's use and perception of the town centre (Southern Tourist Board, 1996, and Ravenscroft and Rowley, 1997), indicate that this influx of leisure property is generally very well received (see **Figure 2**). This is particularly apparent among visitors to the town, who view the increasing choice and diversity of food and beverage outlets as a strong addition to its overall amenity and appeal. In contrast, the 'non-residents' (those living close to Reading but not visiting it on a regular basis) retain a particularly negative view, based predominantly on perceptions of the town centre as it used to be (Ravenscroft and Rowley, 1997).

Figure 1:   Leisure as a percentage of all property

		% leisure 1985	% leisure 1995	% leisure 1997	% change 1985 — 1997
1.	Broad Street	3	1	3	0
2.	Broad Street Mall (ground)	3	0	0	-3
3.	Broad Street Mall (first)	4	4	4	0
4.	Friar Street	16	17	17	+1
5.	Union Street Queen Victoria Street	7	9	10	+3
6.	King's Road	3	7	11	+9
7.	Friars Walk	0	0	0	0
8.	Station Road/ Hill/Approach	17	25	27	+10
9.	East Friar Street Cross Street Market Place King Street	15	13	17	+10
10.	West Street Oxford Road Cheapside	16	14	17	+1
11.	London Street	9	10	11	+2
12.	St Mary's Butts Gun Street	21	32	35	+14
13.	King's Walk	N/A	0	14	+14

Figure 2:   Opinions of leisure establishments in the town centre — mean scores

	local residents	day visitors	staying visitors	non-residents	total
evening entertainment	2.54	2.48	3.00	2.72	2.56
places to eat/drink (day)	2.80	2.93	2.97	2.38	2.81
places to eat/drink (evening)	2.77	2.77	2.79	2.18	2.69
overall 'opinion' score	2.70	2.73	2.92	2.43	2.69

Where 4 = very good; 3 = good; 2 = fair; 1 = poor

Further evidence of the overall improvements in the perception of the town centre is contained in a recent survey considering the impact of Closed Circuit Television (CCTV) in the town centre (Markwell, et al, 1997). Over two-thirds of respondents to this survey (those currently visiting the town centre) considered the quality of the town centre to be improving, with over 80 per cent feeling safe when shopping alone during the day, even prior to the introduction of CCTV. Perceptions about personal safety in the evening were less favourable, however, particularly among women and youth and, more generally, among those living in Reading. Indeed, in a recent survey of people's fear of crime (Ravenscroft and Rowley, 1997), youths rated the town centre as the least safe place to be at any time of day or night (**Figure 3**).

Figure 3:   Feelings of safety when alone

	adults, daytime	youth, daytime	adults, after dark	youth, after dark
in your home	3.52	3.51	3.31	3.1
in your neighbourhood	3.33	3.25	2.91	2.76
in your car	3.24		2.84	
on public transport	3.03	2.98	2.35	1.77
in the town centre	2.88	2.76	2.07	1.69
in local parks and playgrounds	2.80	2.77	1.87	1.8
overall 'safety' score	3.13	3.09	2.56	2.11

Scoring system: 4 = very safe, 3 = quite safe,
                   2 = quite unsafe, 1 = very unsafe

At present, it is apparent that this felt lack of safety in the town centre after dark is not having a major spatial impact on people's lives. Few men or women yet consider that their concerns about the possibility of becoming a victim of crime influence their lives on a regular basis (see **Figure 4**). However, women in particular state that they 'sometimes' take their concerns into account when deciding on whether or not to visit leisure attractions in the town centre in the evening, whereas they 'rarely' do so in other parts of their lives, whether related to social or work functions.

As a consequence, most people still avoid the town centre after dark and continue to feel threatened by groups of people hanging around in parts of the centre. While the possibility of theft is the principal concern for most shoppers, concerns about the possibility of being a victim of violent crime, particularly involving sexual assault or racial harassment are not as high (**Figure 5**). The greatest fears are expressed by those in the upper age range, from 35 onwards. Respondents in the age group 35-44 express the highest level of fear and show the most concern of becoming a victim of all crime, while the youngest (16-24) and oldest groups (aged over 65) claim to be 'quite concerned' about violent attack.

In general, respondents indicated that they felt safer in the presence of other people, both during the day and at night. This apparent relationship between the presence of people and increasing feelings of safety is one of the prime benefits of encouraging more leisure-related development (Montgomery, 1995a). However, as far as Reading is concerned, increasing numbers of people are not limited to the evenings, but are apparent throughout the day. Indeed, two of the largest increases in pedestrian flows, between 1994 and 1997, have taken place in St Mary's Butts and Market Place/East Friar Street, the areas witnessing the greatest influx of leisure property (**Figure 6**).

Figure 4:   Effect of crime concerns on males and females

	males	females
visits to pubs/clubs/other evening entertainment in the town centre	2.43	2.82
use of local parks and playgrounds	2.25	2.68
life of family	2.24	2.22
social life	2.08	2.3
leisure activities	1.97	2.2
shopping trips to town centre	1.97	2.1
home life	1.94	2.06
travel to/from work or school	1.72	1.89
work	1.80	1.75
average 'crime concern' score	2.04	2.22

Scoring system: 4 = often, 3 = sometimes, 2 = rarely, 1 = never

Figure 5: Concern about possibility of being victim of crime

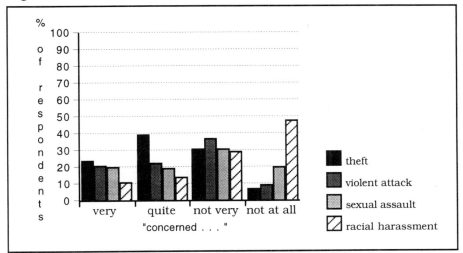

Figure 6: Reading town centre pedestrian flow indices

Area	1987	1991	1994	1997
1. Broad Street	105	94	100	104
2. Friar Street	60	50	54	40
3. Union Street Queen Victoria Street	29	37	44	40
4. East Friar Street, Cross Street, Market Place	27	27	29	36
5. St Mary's Butts	47	33	30	38
6. Station Road/Hill/ Approach	not available			
7. King's Road	24	28	26	26
8. West Street Oxford Road	35	40	38	40
9. London Street	not available			
10. Broad Street Mall (ground)	43	45	76	80
11. Broad Street Mall (first)	36	38	42	37
12. King's Walk	not available		5	22
13. Friars Walk	33	23	27	17

Where Broad Street 1994 is indexed at 100
Note: there is some doubt about the accuracy of the counts for King's Walk and Friars Way

Although the individual frequency of visits to leisure properties remains low (Figure 7), the indications are that town centre users are increasingly being attracted into these 'secondary locations' for purposes other than shopping, particularly to visit cafes, bars and other leisure facilities, with the result that two leisure 'quarters', or 'nodes' are developing around the prime shopping area of the town.

**Figure 7:   Use of leisure premises in Reading's town centre —
mean scores**

	local residents	day visitors	staying visitors	non-residents	total
arts and leisure venues	1.17	0.87	0.35	0.70	0.92
evening entertainment	1.03	0.62	0.50	0.73	0.78
cinemas	0.94	0.49	0.90	0.46	0.66
bars and pubs (day)	0.88	0.41	0.70	0.35	0.57
restaurants and pubs (evening)	1.19	0.64	1.35	0.50	0.83
cafes and restaurants (day)	2.23	2.55	2.27	1.13	2.03
overall 'frequency of use' score	1.24	0.88	1.06	0.62	0.97

Where   5 = one or more times a week; 4 = once a fortnight;
             3 = once a month; 2 = every few months; 1 = rarely; 0 = never

Analysis

At one level, these findings suggest that the health of Reading town centre is improving, underpinned by an apparently symbiotic relationship between retail and leisure premises. However, this neither allows for, nor explains, the dynamics of this shift away from the earlier predominance of retail property. Applying the full set of vitality and viability indicators suggested by the DOE (1996) provides a different interpretation. Using indexed data for property yields, rents, occupancy rates and the proportion of comparison properties, an 'indicator grid' was generated to provide evidence of the changing relative health of the different areas of the town centre, both latitudinally across the town, and longitudinally over time.

While broadly illustrating a distance decay function from the prime areas outwards, the findings indicated that while the health of the prime areas has remained relatively unchanged over the survey period, a marked decline has been witnessed elsewhere in the centre. It is also clear that the distance decay function has become more significant over the survey period, with the relative health of the secondary locations declining significantly over the study period.

Reading's recent apparent increase in both viability and vitality following the economic slump of the early 1990s has thus been highly spatially-specific, leading to the increasing concentration of prime retail outlets at the western end of Broad Street. What is equally apparent is that the areas suffering most in health terms, notably east Friar Street, Market Place and St Marys Butts, for example, are the very places now being colonised by leisure properties. This tends to indicate that the growth of leisure attractions has been driven more by the supply of available properties than by increases in consumer demand, thus effectively excluding the leisure quarters from the revised spatial definition of the core town centre area.

In interpreting these data, therefore, it is apparent that the driving force in this increasing differentiation is the expectation of both property investors and occupiers, defined largely in terms of property yields. These yields quantify the relationship between the capital and rental values of property, with investors (those owning the properties) prepared to accept smaller yields as the security of their investment improves. As the grid indicates, the most secure investments in the town centre are the prime retail sites at the western end of Broad Street, with yields currently around five per cent per annum. These increase rapidly away from this area, with secondary locations in Reading often having yields in excess of 10 per cent per annum, reflecting a large degree of risk associated with letting property (see **Figure 8**, page following).

The primary consequence of this type of yield gradient and its associated reflection of risk is that quality shops seek to relocate to prime areas, other shops cease to trade as the level of retail-related customer flow declines and, in an attempt to maintain property occupation, landlords revise their capital valuations and reduce rents to attract tenants, predominantly from outside the retail sector. It is this process which has provided the opportunity for the influx of leisure property into Reading town centre, with rents now well below those passing in the prime retail areas, and with landlords prepared to accept much higher levels of risk than in the past.

Rather than the influx of leisure properties reflecting the health of the town centre, therefore, it is certainly arguable that they reflect the opposite, particularly the inability of the town to sustain a large-scale prime retail centre. As such, the leisure quarters are more a reflection of opportunism, with landlords seeking to gain some rental income during this period of change, and tenants seeking to capitalise on low rents to develop businesses which could not sustain the full costs of prime town centre property occupation. As such, evidence from the case study appears to support the theorisation that an influx of town centre leisure properties is not necessarily a signification of the increasing health of the town centre.

**Figure 8:   An Index of Commercial Yields for
                 Reading Town Centre**

Area		Yield index (mid 1980s)	Yield index (early 1990s)	Yield index (mid 1990s)
1.	Broad Street		111	100
2.	Friar Street	79	74	65
3.	Union Street Queen Victoria Street			62
4.	East Friar Street Cross Street King Street Market Place	69	74	62
5.	Minster Street Gun Street St Mary's Butts			56
6.	Station Road/ Approach/Hill		62	62
7.	King's Road	93		69
8.	Cheapside Oxford Road West Street	56		50
9.	London Street	69	74	46
10.	Broad Street Mall ground floor	74	74	69
11.	Broad Street Mall first floor	74	74	69
12.	King's Walk	not available	51	46
13.	Friars Walk	69	69	62

   While activity in the town centre demonstrates this proliferation of
predominantly small-scale leisure properties within specific areas, Reading
also has a range of both well-established and new out-of-town leisure
complexes, such as the Showcase multiplex cinema complex at Winnersh on
the south eastern edge of the town, the recent opening of a David Lloyd Sports
Centre at the Thames Valley Business Park immediately east of the town
centre and a number of mixed retail/leisure complexes, such as Pincents
Lane, on the western peripheries of the town and including the Utopia
nightclub, and the new Basingstoke Road retail park with associated themed
food outlets.

In each of these cases, with large sites containing a ..umber of separate leisure businesses (often including service elements such as food and beverages), the developers have been able to make use of planning consents achieved prior to the latest revision of PPG6 (DOE, 1996). In effect, these sites share much in common, apart from location, with town centres, particularly with respect to the benefits of complimentarity in attracting large numbers of customers, with diversity in having prime attractions associated with secondary services and, increasingly, by being accessible via a range of public and private transport mediums.

The level of available property-related detail about these leisure sites is considerably less than that available in the town centre, primarily because they tend to be in single ownership and tend not to have been traded since first being acquired. In their recent work, however, St Quintin (1997) indicate that in the period from the beginning of 1993 to late 1996, yields on such leisure park developments improved from approximately 10 per cent per annum (similar to the current yields being obtained in the emerging town centre leisure 'quarters') to a little over seven per cent per annum (similar to the current yields being obtained on the margins of the prime town centre retail area).

Implications and conclusions

This work is still at an early stage, dealing with a fast evolving situation in which the locational determinants of property occupiers are increasingly being influenced by factors beyond market demand. In particular, the increasing interest in town centre management, together with planning policies seeking to halt decentralisation, has certainly contributed to the encouragement of leisure-related development in many town centres. Indeed, in the aftermath of the economic slump of the early 1990s, with stagnation in retail sales, many local authorities have placed increasing reliance on the development of an alternative economic base, focused not only on leisure attractions, but also on extending the commercial operation of their town centres to cover evenings and weekends.

Concurrently investors, formerly distrustful of any properties deriving their value principally from their occupants rather than their location, have found that certain types of leisure property, in certain associations and locations, could make attractive investment propositions:

> The leisure sector is a rapidly evolving and dynamic part of the property market which has recently emerged as a significant focus of investor interest (St Quintin, 1997: p. 3)

To this extent, at least, it would appear that Reading is taking on some of the principal characteristics of the mixed-use, multi-functional compact city increasingly at the centre of UK and European urban policy. How far this reflects either the explicit impact of coherent policy formulation, or the emergence of an identifiable process of postmodernisation, is open to debate.

In policy terms it is certainly questionable how far the local authority has been influential. Indeed, following Critcher's (1992) critique of Sheffield and the World Student Games, it is equally questionable how far it actually has the capacity to be influential, given the primacy and increasing globalisation of markets, even for locationally-specific products such as property.

Rather than the town centre locations favoured by both local and central government, therefore, investors have predominantly been interested in edge-of-town sites with good car access and above ground parking. This has meant that, in the main, town centre leisure properties have tended to be smaller, individual units with neither the commercial viability nor the need to attract external investors. While needing to locate close to potential customers, therefore, these smaller operators have always tended to rely on opportunism, in selecting properties not deemed suited to other, usually retail, uses.

The principal factor behind the increasing collection of these smaller units in centrally-located cultural or leisure quarters is, again, hardly the result of official policy, instead being more related to the traditional reliance on opportunism. However, rather than being solely the preserve of the traders, opportunism has also been displayed by local authorities and town centre managers, in recognising the marketing potential of these areas, in promoting the emergence of the 'postmodern city', even if the underlying economic and social health of the urban area is rather less secure.

Indications from those living in some of Reading's inner city and suburban areas certainly casts doubt on the extent to which the local authority's vision of the development of the town centre as a leisure and cultural attraction can be achieved, certainly in the short-term. Findings from a recent survey, undertaken in a number of neighbourhoods in Reading, on people's fear of crime (Ravenscroft and Rowley, 1997a), suggests that the town centre, particularly after dark, remains the environment in which people, particularly youth, feel least safe.

In addition to this longer term uncertainty about safety, direct threats to the viability of these areas are likely to come from two interrelated forces. The first of these, already being experienced in Reading, is increasing competition among the existing traders causing a high business failure rate and leading to a continuingly low level of permanent property occupation. Given the increasing salience of PPG6, with its authorisation of local government intervention in the land market for the purpose of site assembly, the second threat is that these peripheral areas, with their growing leisure-related identity, could become prime sites for new integrated town centre leisure developments. Examples of this can already be found. New schemes have been developed in Luton, Bexleyheath and Wolverhampton with a further one, incorporating a multiplex cinema, family entertainment centre, nightclub and restaurants, recently proposed for an area adjacent to Bromley station (anon, 1997).

Not only is the financial rationale behind these developments different from the types of property they replace, but so is the social context. Whereas the principal behind the evolution of the leisure or cultural quarter is the replication and enhancement of the traditional function of cities as meeting places (Montgomery, 1995), these new developments are based on an assurance of financial and social exclusivity. Complete with CCTV and, increasingly, private security, the function of these types of developments is less to encourage social integration than it is to provide the assurances of safety increasingly perceived to be absent from the wider urban realm.

To an extent, therefore, it can be postulated that, in smaller provincial towns such as Reading, the very success of leisure quarters in generating a mixed use and multi-functional economy may eventually compromise the future of the central area as the hub of the urban environment. For whereas the current occupants of leisure quarters are very much part of a wider, socially accessible, service sector, the new generation of integrated leisure parks are part of an altogether different market in which primary attractions and associated services are brought together in one spatially-contained and centrally controlled location.

While these types of parks remain in suburban and edge-of-town locations central areas will, for the most part, be able to retain their spatial and cultural diversity. As centralising policies such as PPG6 begin to dominate, however, the very impermanence and flexibility which has encouraged small scale leisure attractions to locate in city centres will also facilitate their replacement. In their wake will come the next generation of leisure parks, with their attendant marketing potential as icons of the changing function of city centres, as expressed by the developer of the proposed Bromley scheme:

> This development represents a major opportunity for Bromley to secure a much-needed leisure facility which will become a major landmark leisure and recreational development in the south east. (Leadbetter, 1997: p. 9)

Rather than the development of the evening and 24-hour economy around the emergence of leisure-related areas within town centres reflecting a process of postmodernisation, therefore, it might be argued that the opposite is the case. For whereas these areas essentially replicate the existing functions and diversity of the urban environment, their eventual replacement by sanitised, policed 'leisure parks' will reflect an altogether new and different project.

References

Bach, M. (1997) 'Law of the land', *Leisure Management* Vol. 17, No. 4: pp. 30-31.

Berkshire County Council and Reading Borough Council (1996) *Planning commitments for employment uses at March 1996*. Reading: Reading Borough Council.

Britton, W., Davies, K. and Johnson, T. (1989) *Modern methods of valuation*, 8th edition. London: Estates Gazette.

Carroll, J. (1997) 'All wrapped up in a box', *Leisure Management* 17(3): 12-14.

Comedia (1991) *Out of hours: A study of the economic and social life of town centres*. London: Gulbenkian Foundation.

Commission of the European Communities (1990) *Green Paper on the urban environment*. Brussels: CEC.

Critcher, C. (1992) 'Sporting civic pride: Sheffield and the World Student Games of 1991', in Sugden, J. and Knox, C. (eds) *Leisure in the 1990s: Rolling back the welfare state* (LSA Publication No. 46). Eastbourne: Leisure Studies Association: pp. 193-204.

Department of the Environment (1990) *This common inheritance*. London: HMSO.

————(1994) *UK strategy for sustainable development*. London: HMSO.

———— (1996) *Town centres and retail development. Revised Planning Policy Guidance 6*. London: HMSO.

Department of the Environment and Welsh Office (1993) *Town centres and retail development. Revised Planning Policy Guidance 6*. London: HMSO.

———— (1994) *Transport. Planning Policy Guidance 13*. London: HMSO.

DTZ Debenham Thorpe (1997) *UK leisure parks report*. London: Estates Gazette.

Europroperty (1997) 'Investing in leisure', *Europroperty* Vol. 6, No. 1: pp. 19-27.

Fulford, C. (1995) *PPG13 and the residential developer*. Working Papers in Land Management and Development No 46. Department of Land Management and Development, The University of Reading.

Goad (1985) *Reading Town Centre Shopping Centre Report and Goad Plan*. Hatfield: Charles Goad.

————(1995) *Reading Town Centre Summary Report and Goad Plan*. Hatfield: Charles Goad.

Jacobs, J. (1961) *The death and life of great American cities*. New York: Vintage.

Leadbetter, S. (1997) Quoted in 'Bromley to get MWB complex', *Leisure Opportunities*, Issue 190, 18-31 August 1997, p. 9.

Markwell, S., Rowley, M. and Ravenscroft, N. (1997) *The impact of Closed Circuit Television on perceptions of Reading town centre.* Unpublished report to the Reading CCTV Monitoring Group. Centre for Environment and Land Tenure Studies, The University of Reading

Montgomery, J. (1995) 'The story of Temple Bar: creating Dublin's cultural quarter', *Planning Practice and Research* Vol. 10, No. 2: pp. 135-172.

———— (1995a) 'Urban vitality and the culture of cities', *Planning Practice and Research* Vol 10, No. 2: pp. 101-109.

Property Market Research Services Ltd (1987) *Reading Shopping Flowcount.* Oxford: PMRS.

———— (1991) *Reading Shopping Flowcount.* Oxford: PMRS.

———— (1994) *Reading Shopping Flowcount.* Oxford: PMRS.

Ratcliffe, J. (1978) *An introduction to urban land administration.* London: Estates Gazette.

Ravenscroft, N. (1991) 'The place of leisure facilities in the provision of public leisure services', *Journal of Property Research* Vol. 8, No. 3: 253-269.

———— (1992) *Recreation planning and development.* London: Macmillan.

Ravenscroft, N. and Rowley, M. (1997) *Perceptions and use of Reading's town centre: non-residents' survey.* Unpublished report to Reading Borough Council. Centre for Environment and Land Tenure Studies, The University of Reading.

———— (1997a) *Resident perceptions of the fear of crime in Reading.* Unpublished report to the Safer Reading Campaign. Centre for Environment and Land Tenure Studies, The University of Reading.

Ravenscroft, N., Rowley, M. and Markwell, S. (1997) *Measuring the health of Reading's town centre. Research Series 97/1.* Centre for Environment and Land Tenure Studies, The University of Reading.

Ravenscroft, N., Stevens, T. and Reeves, J. (1997) 'Planning for sport and recreation: implications for the review of PPG17', *Journal of Planning and Environment Law* [1997] pp. 699-705.

Reading Borough Council (1995) *Reading Trends.* Reading: Reading Borough Council.

———— (1996) *Planning Commitments for Employment Uses.* Reading: Reading Borough Council.

St. Quintin (1997) *A review of leisure park development in the UK.* London: St. Quintin.

Southern Tourist Board (1996) *Reading Visitor Survey 1996: Draft Report.*

Southampton: STB.

Stapleton, T. (1986) *Estate management practice*, 2nd edition. London: Estates Gazette.

Urban and Economic Development Group (1994) *Vital and viable town centres: meeting the challenge.* London: HMSO.

Williamson, H. (1994) 'Law affecting leisure property', in Marshall, H. and Williamson, H. (eds) *Law and valuation of leisure property.* London: Estates Gazette: pp. 1-75.

The Myth of the 24-hour City

John Spink and Peter Bramham

Leeds Metropolitan University

> European cities like Leeds should be places of innovation and oppor-
> tunity where people from all different ways of life are thrown together.
> They should be places where horizons are broadened and which act
> as magnets to their surrounding regions. A big city like Leeds should
> be a kaleidoscope of colour and vitality, a theatre of unscripted
> spectacle and drama. (Councillor Jon Trickett, Leader of Leeds City
> Council, 1995)

Several provincial British cities have attempted image transformation by
aiming to develop and present themselves as '24-hour cities'. This paper
explores the nature of the changes sought and achieved within Leeds and
examines the gap between the initial vision and the reality in the use of
leisure time as a significant factor within civic transformation and urban
regeneration.

Like any urban policy initiative these actions can be characterised as
moving from initial vision, through action to implement change, to the final
stages when changes have been realised. This paper will examine Leeds as
a 24-hour city along the traditional lines of policy formation, implementation
and evaluation:

1. Policy and Planning for the 'living city'
2. Deregulation and promotion for the 'fun city'
3. Management and Surveillance of the 'Boys' Zone'

Stage 1: Policy and planning for the 'living city'

In the early 1990s city politicians published a whole raft of consultative policy
developments to take Leeds into the next century. Glossy mission statements
sought to flesh out the slogan 'Leeds City Council-Building for the Future'

with an Urban Development Plan, A Green Strategy for the City, An Economic Strategy, A Transport Strategy as well as detailed policies for urban regeneration, community development, and tourism. Many policies were driven by central government policy agendas, redevelopment agencies and task forces but a distinctive element of local policy was the Leeds 24-hour Initiative.

The initial vision, essential for any planned change, envisaged a 24-hour city through the imagery of sophisticated leisure activities and the promotion of urbane free time to assist the transformation of the down-town area. The images, transmitted through civic officials and politicians in the early 1990s were of an integrated cosmopolitan set of urban lifestyles set in an exciting ambiance of the hedonism of a postmodern city environment, where commerce and culture are intertwined (Rojek, 1995). UK city centres were routinely cast as closed, uninviting, dead spaces in stark contrast to the cultured vitality of cafe society in key European cities. Indeed the two major icons of the promotional material for the 24-hour city were pictures of politicians chatting and sipping coffee at pavement cafes or young business executives enjoying the many themed pubs in the city core. The potentialities which were to be developed were for a 'living city' into which people were naturally drawn as a place of leisure and recreation but also work and residence.

A key feature of the europeanisation and cosmopolitan nature of the change has throughout been the attempt to increase the resident population of city centres from the minimal residential figures still inhabiting them by the 1980s. In Leeds' case merely 900 were recorded (from a metropolitan district population of over 700,000) as occupying downtown wards of the city as a consequence of postwar generations of town and country planning and suburban aspirations which had led to continuing central housing redevelopment and decentralisation. This achieved its apotheosis with the wholesale demolition of the Quarry Hill flats, a huge 'utopian' self-contained urban community built in the 1930s in the heart of the city to house 3,000 workers and their families (Ravetz, 1974). Ironically in the late 1970s, the site and people were cleared to make way for the development of a cultural quarter of the city — a major site for the West Yorkshire Playhouse, the Leeds College of Music as well as Quarry House, the regional home of the NHS Executive and Benefits Agency. Symbolically, the City of Leeds School, the only remaining major secondary school in the heart of the city, was relocated to a green field site away from the city centre some 3 years ago.

The 'living city' visionary element thus attempted to integrate working. shopping, leisure and residence as essential elements of an 'organic' whole which ensured an affluent local population to bring life to the formerly deserted cores of these '9-5' centres. These growing local populations were intended to provide a local market for the consumption of services and by their choice of a central city residential location were expected to match the imagery of a sophisticated metropolitan group of consumers who were affluent, achievers at work and cosmopolitan consumers in their stylish leisure time activities. Cultural activities at weekends and 'bridging' events in the afternoons and early evenings were conceived as attractive devices to encourage the 100,000 workers to linger on in the city rather than rushing home for 'tea' after work. Such a market matched the vision of city centres as exciting places with all-night arts venues, cafe society and a clientele possessing economic and cultural capital (Bourdieu, 1984) to enjoy and invoke a wide range of fashionable and stylish entertainments and activities in a developing downtown.

The 'living city' ideal was essentially integrational and envisaged that once such a market of local residents was established then a broader range of leisure activities would prove much more attractive than suburbia to many singles and couples within the city. An ambiance of pavement cafes, theatre and music venues, attractive piazzas and traffic-free streets presented a significant transformation of leisure opportunities within provincial cities and this was to be associated with a transformation of their resident populations. The redevelopment of derelict sites and buildings into converted lofts, warehouses and penthouses would provide appropriate attractive living spaces. The prospect of a transformative power which was social, economic and physical in effects was one of the factors encouraging civic politicians in their support for the 24-hour city as a living entity. Politicians also felt that such transformations were necessary to attract regional, national and international business to relocate to the North and to Leeds in particular. In the early 1990s there were many notable successes such as Asda, DHSS, First Direct and politicians instinctively felt that the cultural and retailing vitality of Leeds were crucial factors in attracting businesses to relocate and new business to open up in Leeds. A third beneficiary of such developments was city centre tourist destinations and the City Council invested heavily in Gateway Yorkshire, a tourist information service, located at Leeds City Station and geared up to promote Leeds' tourist attractions and guide tourists to the diverse and developing tourist venues within the city and its surrounding environment.

Philosophically, the political vision of the 24-hour city probably had its roots in the left post-Fordist (Henry, 1993) campaigns conducted by the late GLC and other cities, like Sheffield and Liverpool, as early as the 1980s, when faced by Thatcherite welfare retrenchment and deindustrialisation. In some cities, Labour parties fell under the control of younger career politicians keen to break with the defensive staid policies of a trade union-led Labour party and eager to seek new alliances with neglected disadvantaged groups and through new popular cultural forms rather than the more circumspect traditional engines of sports, recreation and arts policies. This new 'socialist' politics sought to be one of active political citizenship and inclusion. An important theme was to include local people in local life and decision-making. Local people should regain control of public spaces and have a presence in public life. Such new politics was also strongly multicultural, drawing from new urban movements around issues of race/ethnicity, gender/sexuality, the environment and importantly, unemployment. Its political focus hoped to mobilise ethnic minorities, women, the elderly — all silent voices in traditional Labour politics, by using accessible popular cultural forms — film, events, festivals and pop concerts. Another important radical thread to policy was the emphasis on environmentally sustainable and healthy cities with a growing focus upon public transport systems and regulation of the private car and urban road expansion.

Cultural transformation had been an engine of change promoted by the work of Worpole and Mulgan (1985), Bianchini *et al.* (1993) and many others, associated with the left-of-centre DEMOS think tank, as capable of bringing positive benefits to former industrial centres and their populations. Cities needed to be creative for a variety of political, cultural, social and economic reasons. As regards the 24-hour city, Worpole recognised that anything beyond 11pm was probably too ambitious (Worpole, 1991), though the public library with its diverse services, symbolised an accessible healthy public space open all hours to all citizens.

It was also the inclusive universalism of the 24-hour city which provided its appeal to politicians and officers:

> The 24 hour city was built on consensus — Trickett, Chamber of Commerce, Chief Constable Hellawell — all the great and the good were there. No one would want to criticise it; no one could challenge the policy — it is universal. We all want safer cities, we all want more trade and employment, we all want more housing. It was not a political thing — it was more a social thing.... (Local government officer, interview August 1997)

However, by the late 1990s right post-Fordist Labour councils like Leeds had developed cultural transformation ideas in association with private investors. Political aspirations of civic inclusion were mediated by the economic reality of private sector partnerships. Such partnerships involved some of the large volume house-building contractors and others included leisure organisations, mostly the large brewery chains. The cultural, community-based inclusive ideals of the left became supplanted by a more exclusive metropolitan vision of the 24-hour city as a venue of highly commodified consumption, a vision further blurred by the wish to develop the tourist gaze and tourist visitors within the city.

The emphasis on style and fashion and consumption clearly integrated these ideas for down-town transformation with the changed political and economic context of the postmodern city in the 1990s (Bramham and Spink, 1994). The vision for change fitted the civic leadership ideals of a number of city bosses and within Leeds was vigorously supported by John (later Jon) Trickett as Leader of the Labour group on the City Council. With that influential leadership and a small policy task force[1], the mechanisms of civic policy support were mobilised to engineer the necessary changes to transform the mundane 9 to 5 provincial city into the image of an exciting and stylish 24-hour city which was an essential adjunct to and expression of post-industrial economic change.

In the words of the council's own publicity material:

> The 24-hour city is for everybody. The purpose is to maximise the potential of the City's economy whilst at the same time enhancing the quality of life of its citizens. (XXIV Twenty Four Hour City Leeds 1995)

Stage 2: Deregulation and promotion for the 'fun city'

In the changes necessary for the transformation of Leeds into 'fun city' the role of the 'Manchester school' was probably as significant as it was in the early nineteenth century battle for free trade. Manchester's vision of civic transformation was influential on most other provincial cities and the flattery by imitation reflects the adoption of Grahame Stringer's foresight in many other locations. A seminal conference in 1993 held at the Institute of Popular Culture, Manchester Metropolitan University (Lovatt, 1994) established the prerequisites for change and promoted the real benefits of a vibrant night-time economy for local domestic products, city multipliers, part-time employment and regional entrepreneurs. Milestone's research (1996) into the youth pop scene in Manchester has documented the central importance of small-scale local businesses and the local media in shaping Manchester's cultural industries quarter. The power of the 24-hour city ideal was thus seen as both intangible in its positive impact on city image but also real in its positive effects on local economies and thus indispensable for 'progressive' right post-Fordist Labour authorities by the mid 1990s.

The Manchester conference of 1993 was attended by John Trickett and many of its suggested initiatives were avidly accepted into the Leeds vision. The debt to Manchester has been informally acknowledged by council officers on the 24-hr city project team which was hurriedly established in Leeds:

> Trickett went to the Manchester conference to talk about retailing but he came away with all the ideas. He didn't just copy them because some of them were already partially mapped out but the Manchester conference was a turning point; it crystalised all his ideas. (Local government officer interview August 1997)

Under Trickett's direct leadership Leeds began a series of initiatives directed at the transformation of the central city. Manchester had made much of its deregulation of traditional leisure activities and the links between licensing and civic license were seen as fundamental. Copying the Manchester experience, which claimed a reduction in drunkenness offences linked to deregulation of some licensing arrangements and an extension of drinking times, Leeds proceeded to change its attitude to the leisure activities of the city centre from the old municipal Labourist puritan regulationist approach to one of an enabler. Under the leadership of Councillor Lorna Cohen (the 'Council's disco-loving granny', YEP, 1994[2]) the Leeds City Licensing

Committee increased licensing hours for 40 night clubs and bars. Many 'cafe bars' and 'disco bars' provide food and entertainment and have become 'watering holes' for those can afford to stay out in exotic places such as Cuban Heels, The Observatory, Cafe Mex and Jumping Jacks.

The Sunday taboo on shopping was shattered in 1995 with the launch of 'Funday, Sunday'. In recent years, the City Council has provided an array of events -largely free for local people and visitors to enjoy. It is in this domain of policy that left post-Fordist ideals of inclusion and public participation are visibly realised. The Council's annual 'Live at Leeds' programme included free opera, jazz, street carnival and ballet. Special street entertainment festival — 'Music, Fire and Masks' entertained visiting football fans during Euro 96. Within the city centre itself, the West Yorkshire Playhouse's 'Rhythms of the City' festival regularly 'brings the city alive with jugglers, dancers, mime artists, actors and singers during the summer'. Over the August Bank Holiday, there is the 'Leeds Waterfront Festival' centred on Granary Wharf, Tetley's Brewery Wharf and Clarence Dock, home of the Royal Armouries.

Civic authorities were seen as holding a key role in the promotion of Leeds as a 24-hour city. The changes were widely publicised, particularly in local TV appearances by key councillors with leisure policy briefs. New night clubs blossomed — the Majestyk (City Square), Nato (Boar Lane), Europa (New Briggate), the Underground, Planet Earth and the Cockpit. The Break for the Border group have acquired the Music Factory club on the corner of Call Lane/Briggate for its first themed restaurant, bar/night club outside London and Dublin. The £3mill. investment will provide a capacity for 1,300 people. The cafe culture saw the opening of half a dozen new establishments including Moderno, Cafe Junction, Cafe Express, Cuban Heels, Arts Cafe, Ruskins, Lillywhites's LW sports cafe and Harvey Nicol's own cafe. Thus, a key element in the fun city campaign was press reporting of the transform-ation. Council officers encouraged national press coverage in an effort to keep pace with venues like Newcastle and Manchester, seen as direct competition, and Leeds began to generate national notice as a 'swinging city' and 'a city that never sleeps'.

Much of this was illusory and concerned 'talking a good game' in Man-chester's view. Perhaps more substantial was the change of climate developed within the city planning department with the growth of a more positive attitude towards an integrated city with support for mixed-use development, recognition of the symbiotic leisure use of 'backland', basement or upper-floor retail spaces and more sympathetic approach to entrepreneurial initiatives. Such intangibles have effected change in layout and composition of the down-town core and have led to more diverse patterns of central land uses within which leisure figures strongly.

Stage 3: Reality — management and surveillance of 'boys' zone'

Extension of civic license and the carnivalesque may thus be seen to fit the transforming postindustrial provincial city and the nature of postmodern hedonistic lifestyles, but there clearly is a cost to such initiatives. Leeds was prepared to spend extensively on civic facelifts for its pedestrianised core and Landmark Leeds scheme in paving and planting to attract shoppers and business. The emphasis has been on safer, more comfortable walks[3], as well as an investment in stylish street furniture[4]. Keeping the 24-hour fun city safe, attractive and accessible has presented another set of problems. In an effort to cope with extended night time activity there has been an investment in lighting[5] and, although the last of British cities to install it (Graham, Brooks and Heery, 1996), closed circuit camera surveillance. All has been developed in Trickett's terms:

> A well used city- day and night- that is safe, accessible and friendly
> to all ages and walks of life is the Council's ultimate goal. (Press
> Release: The Leeds 24 Hour City Initiative March 1997)

Echoes of civic regulation have always been linked to fears over leisure excesses and the disorder associated with city centres at night. A key adjunct to any 24-hour city project has been consideration of the licensing of the populace enjoying the excitements on offer. The contradictions of deregulation and control lie at the heart of this issue and high technology through CCTV[6] has been one of the ways in which the paradox has been resolved, at least partially and relatively unobtrusively.

But the issue of control and surveillance in all its Foucauldian immensity remains a real one for 24-hour cities. High technological solutions of policing city centres can often be illusory and may run counter to long-term community-based policing. During the 1970s and 1980s, there have been fierce debates about the policy tension between 'reactive' coercive policing and 'crime fighting' and more 'proactive' community styles of law enforcement. A specialised professionalised police force, sustained by high technological support, can distance themselves from the wider communities they are empowered to serve. These dilemmas are cast into sharp relief in the more detached anonymous world of the city centre after dark, full of non-local pleasure seekers.

Research on law enforcement suggests that the 'working personality' of the police in city centres is one of dealing with crime 'hot-spots', informed by stereotypes of citizens which recognise different categories of people who are defined by experience to be 'police property' — those young males who are likely to be violent, criminal, drunk and disorderly, as well as those involved in a myriad of drugs-related offences. All the national research suggest that drugs are a central feature for many involved in city-centre club and rave scene and that inner-city communities struggle to cope with the vicissitudes of hard-drug distribution and consumption patterns. Leeds as a city is no exception and has a major drugs project underway in Killingbeck division. Indeed Leeds has a national reputation from recent riots in the Hyde Park student area which has also suffered from national coverage for rapes, violent crime and homicide. The working style of policing is one of vigilance which sits uncomfortably within a wider 24-hour city policy of relaxed indulgence.

So, the reality for Leeds had been that despite investment in the West Yorkshire Playhouse and the retention of national players like Jude Kelly as artistic director, the development of initial contemporary dance strengths in Chapeltown/Harehills, there has been relatively little flowering of culture and the arts in the downtown at night[7]. The *Architect's Journal* (May 1997) recently commented that the deregulation of the city's culture had actually led to a proliferation of bars and other venues associated with alcohol. Despite these being themed, sophisticated and attractive during the day to the cultural capitalists of the business world, by night their clientele remains almost exclusively within the youth market. In many cases the city council and its planning teams seem to have preferred association with the certainties of large-scale brewery developers rather than the uncertainties of reliance on small-scale entrepreneurs (Architects Journal: May 1997). The result has been a massive investment in bars and clubs usually linked with multi-national brewing concerns[8]. Downtown now boast bars and clubs which attract an exclusively youth clientele every evening.

Observers like Irena Bauman (Architect's Journal, May 1997) and a recent report from the Chamber of Commerce have noted that the downtown was not for them. The prevalence of alcohol and other drugs has ensured that the central city streets become dominated by crowds of young people, mostly men. at midweek and every weekend[9]. The night-time economy is thus buoyant at least until 2.00 a.m. There are many more venues open, the image of the city to young people is positive and attractive, the pubs and clubs are well regulated. The city ideals of partnerships extend to the policing of private and public spaces. Four hundred door staff have recently completed a city council-run training programme and provide security for the private spaces of the clubs and bars. Over a thousand people are officially registered to work as door staff in licensed premises throughout Leeds. Disorderly consumers are thrown out onto the streets like rubbish and are excluded from other venues. The public streets still remain the domain of constabulary forces, sometimes supported by local council programmes and staffing such as Leedswatch[10].

However, this prosperous city-centre night life differs markedly from the vision of the inclusive sophisticated 24-hour city. The reality is much more segregated and highly selective by age, gender and ethnicity. It is principally alcohol fuelled leading to squalid provincial delinquency and disorder rather than the initial prospect of cosmopolitan urbanity. Domination by young people effectively marks a social, economic and cultural closure of the centre to others. In social terms, domination by the young (under 35 yrs) white alcohol drinkers restricts access by older people, women, ethnic groups and other interlopers into a set of local gang 'turfs' which have been established, often related to city districts and territories. The streets are sites and sights for the display of particular forms of aggressive hegemonic masculinity. The 'lads' are cheery but violent, displaying a physicality which ignores the cold climate, as they noisily cruise their established route from one venue to another through the city. 'Suitable' young women are tolerated within the core, but again with a minimalist and fashionable dress sense which celebrates gender differences! The aim is to 'get pissed' and at the end of the night out 'to pull'. This establishes a segregative exclusivity in which this version of the 24-hr city becomes a repellent reality for others.

Instead of the multi-functional cultural diversity envisaged by its architects, the Leeds night scene is about extensive alcohol consumption and clubbing. Music venues and bars are dominated by the multi-national large-scale entrepreneurs rather than localized initiatives. Rather than 24-hour activity the city is now dead by 2.00 a.m. since the economics of staffing limit any greater extension of hours. The dead hours of the city are recast as dead drunk hours, with consumers running out of money and steam. It is not a croissant one is nibbling in a cafe at 5 o'clock in the morning (as envisaged in the publicity literature) but something 'meaty' from a mobile burger stall at half-past two before falling into a taxi.

Earlier studies (Bramham and Spink, 1994) have noted the perceptions of wider citizenry of the city centre at night as predominantly those of fear. The last couple of years have seen a number of violent and even fatal incidents which have served to reinforce such perceptions. These incidents, well publicised within the local media, have reinforced the avoidance of central areas by other groups and confirmed the city core as an exclusive 'boys' zone' with all that entails for drunkenness, violent crime, litter and petty but expensive vandalism.

Policing the city centre core is expensive. The Millgarth division (at the heart of the city centre) consumes six times more resources per capita than any other police division within the city. The allocation of resources is based upon a Home Office formula calculated in relation to a variety of factors, residential and transient populations, demographic makeup, social and economic factors. The important point to remember is that the Millgarth Division's budget had remained stationary over the past three years despite the increased policing requirements of the 24-hour city initiative since 1994.

The higher investment in resources only yields the average level of crime detection, a rate of 25 per cent for the whole city. Despite other divisions having many times more population[11], Millgarth has the highest number of recorded crimes — particularly violent crimes and vehicle thefts (see **Table 1** following page).

Civic resources have not expanded to keep pace with the extended working day of the centre. The police must maintain vigilance and control for longer periods, city cleansing teams have more litter, through night-time generated drinking and fast food outlets and public transport has not been

Table 1:   West Yorkshire Police Authority; Policing Plan 1996/97, Leeds Metropolitan District

Police Division	Population	Budget £ 000s	Expenditure per capita	Ratios of expenditure
1. Chapeltown	98,168	£7,380	£ 75.17	1.51
2. Holbeck	137,862	£8,308	£ 60.26	1.21
3. Killingbeck	151,839	£8,964	£ 59.03	1.18
4. Millgarth	25,413	£7,907	£311.13	6.25
5. Pudsey	111,493	£5,961	£ 53.46	1.07
6. Weetwood	155,115	£7,717	£ 49.75	1.00

able to service the deregulated transport environment. The result has been exclusive in every sense and encourages the conspicuous discretionary expenditure of the young, rather than the cultured sophistication of the hoped-for middle class residents. The city centre has not become more accessible at night for the majority of citizens, quite the reverse.

In many ways the original 'organic' vision of the city for residence, work and leisure has been lost. Although the original figure of 900 population has increased, perhaps to 4,000, the numbers in reality have been swollen by the exploitation of multi-functional buildings by students and the single young and by the construction of student residences and housing association single-person units. This expansion of the resident population thus serves to reinforce the exclusivity of the core, rather than to encourage diversity. The student lifestyle provides additional economic support for the bars and clubs mid-week and encourages further investment by the larger multi-national enterprises exploiting the youth market. With city council support this reinforcement of a particular form of 'fun city' tends to militate against the cultured vision initially embarked upon by Trickett and the right post-Fordist Labour regime. 'Closure' remains a key concept in examining the transforming city centre and new initiatives suggest that the current emphasis on youth, alcohol and dance clubs is likely to be perpetuated and intensified. The choice of Leeds as 'Sound City 97' is, therefore, no small coincidence.

Conclusion

The focus of the 24-hour city is an important one for leisure studies since it represents a civic policy attempt to use leisure lifestyles for urban regeneration and economic diversification. The distortion of the original conception is significant in policy evolution terms and in its representation of contemporary city centre leisure cultures.

In evaluating the 'boys' zone' created in central Leeds a number of issues are raised. One must be the extent to which this represents a change in gender domination or whether central areas have always tended towards male dominance. Centres may have always have been restrictive and masculine, though perhaps now much more youth centred than ever. Certainly, the ambiance created in the 'fun city' of pubs and clubs is not welcoming to older people and does not serve the original objectives of a place of attractive culture encouraging use by mature, diverse residents and visiting tourists.

One of the unintended consequences of the Leeds 24-hour city initiative is young men's dominance of city leisure space which paradoxically contradicts their loss of dominance of work places with the deindustrialisation of the city. In modernity, the presence of male workers dominated day-light working hours and city centre locations. With the flexibilisation and feminisation of postmodern work processes, young males appear to have become displaced into the exercise of territorial control in the night-time economy. Displays of masculinity and solidarity are no longer experienced in the world of production on the shop floor but are recreated within the bars and clubs as 'the lads' work at their leisure.

The consequent salience of alcohol and resultant latent violence may be a traditional focus, but this seems to be targeted at purely youth markets currently, restricting the wider appeal of the city centre. Whether this is economically and financially beneficial seems to be answered by the continued reinvestments of large brewery and leisure chains and certainly the positive image amongst the youth market seems self-reinforcing and continuingly successful.

The image of an exciting core is at least sustained in media reviews and to that extent must fulfil some of the city policy-makers' objectives. Questions must be raised, however, about the extra municipal costs involved in cleansing, transport, policing and maintenance, and the balance sheet is currently being assembled by city officials as an annual audit of the health of the city. This audit not only surveys economic indicators but also measures transport flows, housing patterns, pollution levels and citizen satisfaction with local services. So far much of the municipal investment and servicing costs appears to benefit large corporate entrepreneurs rather than local traders and the beneficial inputs into the local economy may be restricted through low paid and part-time flexiblised employment patterns. The 24-hour city as currently realised in Leeds for work and play seems to best fit the younger generation of citizens and temporary visitors, mostly students. In terms of the original extended concept of an integrated living city, little seems to have been achieved. For the entire spectrum of citizens, until the attraction of the centre reaches a wider public, the 24-hour city concept must remain more myth than reality for cities.

Notes

1 This policy has been driven by a new City Centre Management Committee and the Press and Public Relations Unit. Both are indicative of new flexible post-Fordist forms of local authority organisation, such as the Leeds Development Agency, set up within the Planning Department. Interestingly local officials were unsure as to who should receive the City Centre 'audit' data. Their destination was thought to be either the Planning Department or the City Centre Management Committee (or both).

2 Lorna Cohen (Lab) is one of the three Leeds Councillors on the West Yorkshire Police Authority. All three Councillors (Colin Campbell: Lib-Dem; Neil Taggart: Lab) have major roles in Leisure Services Committees.

3 5,000 metres of new pavements (including 'new look' projects) and 2000 metres of pavements repaired, 50 new or improved pedestrian crossings.

4 The City has invested in the following since 1993 'nearly 90 new seats, over 300 new litter bins, over 50 styled new bus-shelters(by Metro and Adshel); visitor information: 50 pedestrian finger-sign posts, 20 pictorial visitor maps; extensive flower displays,' flower' fountains and 'arches', fixtures for hanging baskets. Source: Leeds City Centre Briefing, Issue No. 2. March 1997.

5 120 streets with new or improved lighting (86% of all streets); over 300 new lighting columns; nearly 400 lights upgraded. The City Council's 'facelift and lighting' grant programme has resulted in 41 buildings being 'facelifted' and 10 floodlighting schemes completed by the end of 1996.

6 Leedswatch the City Council's £400,000 security surveillance system became fully operation in November 1996. The initial phase included 19 cameras throughout the city centre with electronic link-ups to West Yorkshire Police at Killingbeck as well as the city centre Millgarth station. The next phase of 10 cameras, funded by the Home Office via the Leeds Initiative, will be installed around the Leeds Waterfront.

7 Yorkshire Dance Centre has completed a 11 year building conversion programme of a clothing factory near Quarry Hill at a cost of £1.4mill, supported by Lottery funding.

8 The big brewers Tetley's (Swans, Circus Circus, Scruffy Murphys, the Feast and Firkin and Carpe Diem) and Bass (Sparrow's Wharf, the Dry Dock, the Courtyard, All Bar One and Edwards) have invested millions In the city centre; smaller entrepreneurial initiatives (like Mex, Zacks and Montezumas) have taken off.

9 Several Leeds Metropolitan University students have confirmed these findings in recent dissertations drawing on small exploratory surveys and on ethnographic research.

10 Leedswatch CCTV is to be supplemented by the City Council's own city centre security patrol. Uniformed council staff will deal with illegal street trading and aggressive begging.

11 In relation to the Millgarth Division, Chapeltown (3.9) and Pudsey (4.4) have four times more population; Holbeck (5.4) has five times and Killingbeck (6.0) and Weetwood (6.1) has six times more population.

References

Bianchini, F. and Parkinson, M. (1993) *Cultural policy and urban regeneration: The West European experience*. Manchester University Press.

Bourdieu, P. (1984) *Distinction: A social critique of taste*. London: Routledge.

Bramham, P. and Spink, J. (1994) 'Leisure and the postmodern city', in I. P. Henry (ed) *Leisure: Modernity, post-modernity and lifestyles* (LSA Publication No. 48). Eastbourne: Leisure Studies Association.

Graham, S. Brooks, J. and Heery, D. (1996) 'Towns on the television', *Local Government Studies*, Vol. 22, No. 3: pp. 1-27.

Henry, I. P. (1993) *The politics of leisure policy*. London: MacMillan

Milestone, K. (1996) *Pop scene in Manchester*. Unpublished PhD, Manchester Metropolitan University.

Mulgan, G. and Worpole, K. (1985) *Saturday night or Sunday morning?*. London: Comedia.

Leeds Development Agency (1997) *Leeds City Centre Briefing Issue* No. 2 (March).

Architect's Journal (1997) *Leeds Special Issue* (May).

Lovatt, A. (1994) *The 24-hour city*. Manchester: Institute of Popular Culture, Manchester Metropolitan University.

Ravetz, A. (1974) *Model estate*. London: Croom Helm.

Rojek, C. (1995) *Decentring leisure*. London: Sage.

West Yorkshire Police Authority Policing Plan 1996/97 West Yorkshire Police.

West Yorkshire Chief Constable Annual Report 1996 West Yorkshire Police.

Worpole, K.(1992) *People and towns*. London: Comedia.

Other LSA Publications Volumes

Note: Volumes 1–47 are A4 format. Volumes from No. 48 inclusive are 6x9 inch, perfect-bound. Prices vary according to LSa membership status. Information may be obtained from: LSA PUBLICATIONS c/o the Chelsea School, University of Brighton, Eastbourne BN20 7SP (UK) FAX [0044] (0)1323 644641 E-mail: mcfee@solutions-inc.co.uk

Details of the most recent LSA Publications volumes are are presented on the following pages.

TOURISM AND VISITOR ATTRACTIONS: LEISURE, CULTURE AND COMMERCE

LSA Publication No 61. ISBN: 0 906337 71 2 [1998] pp. 211

Edited by Neil Ravenscroft, Deborah Philips and Marion Bennett

Contents

THE PRODUCTION AND CONSUMPTION OF SPORT CULTURES: LEISURE, CULTURE AND COMMERCE

LSA Publication No. 62. ISBN: 0 906337 72 0 [1998] pp. 178
Edited by Udo Merkel, Gill Lines, Ian McDonald

Contents

GENDER, SPACE AND IDENTITY: LEISURE, CULTURE AND COMMERCE

LSA Publication No. 63. ISBN: 0 906337 73 9 [1998] pp. 191
Edited by Cara Aitchison and Fiona Jordan

Contents

CONSUMPTION AND PARTICIPATION: LEISURE, CULTURE AND COMMERCE

LSA Publication No. 64. ISBN: 0 906337 74 7 [forthcoming 1999]
Edited by Malcolm Foley and Garry Whannel

CONTENTS

LEISURE, TIME AND SPACE: MEANINGS AND VALUES IN PEOPLE'S LIVES

LSA Publication No. 57. ISBN: 0 906337 68 2 [1998] pp. 198 + IV
Edited by Sheila Scraton

Contents